P9-CFS-663

STONEHAM

JUN 0 3 2013

PUBLIC LIBRARY

BEAUTIFUL THING

BEAUTIFUL THING

Inside the Secret World of Bombay's Dance Bars

SONIA FALEIRO

Black Cat
New York

Copyright © 2010 by Sonia Faleiro

All rights reserved. No part of this book may be reproduced in any form or by any electronic or mechanical means, including information storage and retrieval systems, without permission in writing from the publisher, except by a reviewer, who may quote brief passages in a review. Scanning, uploading, and electronic distribution of this book or the facilitation of such without the permission of the publisher is prohibited. Please purchase only authorized electronic editions, and do not participate in or encourage electronic piracy of copyrighted materials. Your support of the author's rights is appreciated. Any member of educational institutions wishing to photocopy part or all of the work for classroom use, or anthology, should send inquiries to Grove/Atlantic, Inc., 841 Broadway, New York, NY 10003 or permissions@groveatlantic.com.

Originally published in India in 2010 by Hamish Hamilton an imprint of Penguin Books India.

First published in Great Britain in 2011 by Canongate Books Ltd. Edinburgh

Printed in the United States of America

ISBN: 978-0-8021-7092-7

Black Cat
a paperback original imprint of Grove/Atlantic, Inc.
841 Broadway
New York, NY 10003
Distributed by Publishers Group West
www.groveatlantic.com

12 13 14 15   10 9 8 7 6 5 4 3 2 1

For Ulrik

'My story is the best you will ever hear.
The best, understand?
Now come close.
Closer!
Okay, ready?'

Contents

PART I
January 2005

'Challenge me. Any man, any time'

Leela told me she was beautiful. And as she assessed herself in front of a full-length mirror in a vest and the boxer shorts of the customer asleep on the bed beside her, I had no reason to disagree.

She wasn't tall, she admitted. And her breasts were make-believe; her bra was 'imported-padded'. Her shoulder-length hair was streaked butterscotch and her eyes, unlike those of any girl from her hometown of Meerut up north, were a velvety mauve you might see in the sky on a day that promised rain. If a customer gestured, '*Asli? Ya nakli?*' Leela would pretend she didn't know he was referring to the colour of her eyes and smirk, until the customer, flooded with nervous excitement, felt like he'd spied something he shouldn't have—the creamy curve of her chocolate breast between the metal hooks of her sari blouse.

But Leela as Leela had been born was in there too, and it was this natural 'booty', 'straight from the hand of God', that she was most proud of. The other girls, she said, were 'black, like Banglas', and once they'd scrubbed their faces clean of the Dreamflower powder without which they wouldn't leave home, they were no prettier than the beggar-monkeys snatching bananas out of the hands of devotees at the Hare Krishna temple down the street.

But not Leela. Stripped of everything, including her knickerbra, she was still a wonder, she said—not unlike the Taj Mahal of Agra city bathed in moonlight.

Although I couldn't attest to all of the above, this much I will say: Leela's face was a perfect heart, the sort style magazines use to demonstrate make-up most suitable for different face shapes. Her hands and feet were shapely and smooth and, like her complexion, of a dark gold. Her bare fingers were tipped with hard, square nails that came in use when the dance floor got too crowded for her liking. And knowing well the elegance of her little nose, Leela would flaunt it like an engagement ring. On certain evenings at the dance bar, when she needed to increase the padding of hundred rupee notes in her bra, Leela would engage only in silhouette.

But beauty wasn't everything. What you wore made the difference between a fifty and a five hundred.

What you said to your customer when he feigned reluctance to spend another evening merely watching you was crucial. So was how you said it. Remember the wise words of the legendary courtesan Umrao? 'No one knows how to love more than we do: to heave deep sighs; to burst into tears at the slightest pretext; to go without food for days on end; to threaten to take arsenic . . .'

Umrao was a beauty, but it was her epic *nakhra*, pretence, that made her legend. Leela understood this immutable fact of her profession and so she stayed sharp, 'sharp,' she said, 'as a double-edged razor blade'.

'Challenge me,' she would say, 'any man, any time. A hi-fi man, *your* kind of man. I'll snap him up, like a fisherman does a pomfret.'

'Challenge me,' she would demand, and on evenings when she talked drunk and stepped funny, when the roots of her hair, black as her real eye colour, showed up disloyally under the twenty-watt bulbs of her 1 Bedroom-Hall-Kitchen flat (BHK), there would be something like hope in her eyes.

Leela asked for trouble because trouble was free.

'Challenge!' Snapping my bra strap.

'Challenge!' Pretending to burn me with the ever-present Gold

Flake between her fingers until I cried out, I believe you, Leela! You will win.

∽

I wasn't being conciliatory. Leela was the winning sort; the kind of girl you wanted by your side when you bought your stack of Friday morning lottery tickets outside Churchgate station.

She won against her lover Purshottam Shetty. The sharp-faced, short-legged, married father of two was her 'husband' and by any standard, even by those of the dance bar, she was his down low. And yet the value of what she received from him, Leela said, like a child insisting to her mother she could play in the rain and not catch cold, exceeded the value of what she gave up to be with him. She won against her mother, Apsara, though Leela's tactics weren't fair. 'Apsara' means 'celestial nymph', but Leela's Apsara weighed over eighty kilograms and had a face like a cutting board. The orange stubs of her teeth stuck so far out they might have belonged to another face. When she spoke, the daughter said of her mother, mother sounded like an audio cassette someone had pressed the fast-forward button on. When she entered a room, Leela turned the screw, it was like night had descended. 'You're so fat!' Leela would screech, caring neither that her joke, if it was that, was amusing, nor that her mother was not amused.

And Leela won against her father Manohar. But that was long after he started renting her out to the *ghodas*, the police, opposite her school. When they took her virginity from her, cursing that she'd knotted the drawstring of her salwar like it was a sack of *atta* she was saving for winter, all she saw were the peepal trees of the station compound. Their leaves had crowded together, it seemed to her, to gossip and wonder at her shame.

When I first met Leela, she was the highest-paid bar dancer in Night Lovers, the dance bar in which she worked, perhaps in all of Mira Road, the Bombay suburb in the crowded midst of which she then lived. I was a reporter researching an article on Bombay's bar dancers. The story wasn't published because it wasn't considered 'newsworthy'. No one wanted to read about a community of marginalized dancing girls who had been around, it seemed, forever. And yet, I found myself making excuses to meet with Leela, again and again.

Let me try to explain why.

Leela was paid to dance for men. And I, and most people I knew, had seen bar dancers only in Bollywood films—not as the protagonist, but as background entertainment, one-dimensional and on the margins; manipulated and mistreated. Because of what I'd seen on film, Leela's success and optimism, her magnetic vivacity, revealed so vividly when we first met, was to me a mysterious thing.

Soon enough, I discovered how truly unlike we were. Leela was a free spirit. She lived by her own moral code; she followed no religious text; and to a customer she might say '*gaand meri chaat*', kiss my ass. She was clearly no saint. But her flaws made her human; even her inconsistencies were beguiling. It took me six months to find out where she'd really been born. She said she was forced to sleep with men for money, even though she made more money than she knew where to hide. She said her feelings for Shetty were the real thing and wondered why he didn't reciprocate in the manner she wished—in the doting, hen-pecked style of the husband character played by Amitabh Bachchan in the film that made her cry all through, *Baghban*.

All Leela wanted, Leela confided with a Meena Kumari in *Pakeezah* sigh, was to fall in love and become a housewife and mother.

From Leela's point of view, our friendship was an adventure. She was seven years younger than me, but only she could teach me what I wanted to know—the truth about a world that fascinated me, intimidated me, and as I came to know it better, left me feeling frustrated and hopeless.

When we first met, I lived in Bombay's Manhattan, in the

southern tip of the city. Some people refer to South Bombay as 'town', a town within the city of Bombay, a place so special it deserves its own borders.

The British stamped South Bombay with regal buildings of limestone domes and sparkling white pillars. South Bombay has sweeping streets that get swept and ancient trees with fan-like leaves flurrying with pigeons. It has the Four Seasons, the Taj that was bombed, the Taj that wasn't. It has sushi restaurants and cafés that bake thirty kinds of fudge brownies. It is owned by men in Cavalli and by women who favour Lanvin; couples who like to inform everyone they meet that *Vogue* magazine once referred to them as 'Bombay's beau monde'.

At the other end of this dazzling spectrum that defined not just South Bombay but India itself were the street kids in their barefooted, dust-smeared scruffiness selling pirated Gladwell, Rowling and Roy at one traffic light and cheekily begging a lift to the next.

Where Leela lived there were no domes, no pillars, no sushi restaurants. You didn't carry a minaudière, you carried a *thaili*, a plastic bag; if you were stylish, a pleather purse with chain links. There were restaurants and hotels, of course, but if you lived outside Mira Road it's unlikely you would've heard of them, or that you would want to stop by.

The view was unusual—salt pans—but it was usual too dinky cars stuttering over potholes, gangs of stray dogs chasing cyclists. Of residential buildings that resembled giant washing lines, their every window, every balcony enclosed by intricate grillwork, giving these buildings the appearance of prisons, and their occupants, when they peered through, appeared imprisoned.

Despite the apparent difference in our worlds, Leela had no curiosity about me. She once asked how much I earned and whether I 'went' with 'boys' and, if so, how much they earned. But she would never know much of my life outside of hers; she wouldn't even know where I lived. Leela didn't know, because Leela didn't listen. Leela wanted only to be heard. And the best way to accomplish that, she knew, was not to change the subject if the subject was her.

So our often one-sided relationship may be characterized thus: I called Leela. She 'missed-called' me.

∽

But for now let us return to that Tuesday fresh in the New Year, when Leela's only worry was that the afternoon would end in a fight. I had dropped by to visit Leela and, having shaken my hand, she motioned silently to the figure sleeping off his excesses. '*Dekho, lund-fakeer*,' she said uncharitably. Check out the sex maniac.

I assessed the man's face—scarred, pouchy, pocked with bristles—the way I might have a small animal discovered under the bed. I didn't get close. I searched for signs of aggression. And I wondered if the man would leave voluntarily, or if Leela and I would have to take advantage of his stupor and kick him out of the flat.

What's his name? I whispered.

Leela shrugged.

What should we do? I prodded.

She yawned.

We might as well have been talking about a stranger.

Then I realized we probably *were* talking about a stranger. Leela almost never asked questions of her customers—they didn't interest her. And as a matter of principle, she always told them lies.

Then I recognized him, or I recognized rather the lumpy scar that ran from the side of his forehead all the way down to his chin. It was a scar Leela liked to believe had been earned in a 'gangvar', tackling an assassin's .45. But if I recalled correctly, curled up before me was the manager of hotel Pure Vegetarian, a man referred to by his waiters as a *bhonsdi ka*, son of a whore, for pinching their tips; a man who had cut himself having fallen off the footboard of the local train attempting to spit out a mouthful of paan. If I was right then I was looking at the man whose wife, Leela and I righteously agreed, was a bit of a *besharam*, a shameless one. When visiting a friend in the building, she sashayed about in a nightgown and slippers, which was regular on their street, but she refused to cover her breasts with a chunni, thus revealing even to Feroze *'Andha'* Bashir, the neighbourhood's cataract-eyed egg seller, that she fancied lime green bras from Thailand.

Leela wanted her customer out because she was 'bijniss'-like. He'd done his bijniss and now, she believed, he should beat it *patli gali se*, by the quickest way. But she was also in a hurry because she had to leave for Night Lovers, which was owned and managed by Shetty.

Because they were 'husband-wife', Leela said to me, she had to be scrupulously professional. She couldn't be late. But neither would she leave a customer in her flat, even though she referred to this particular customer as *bhai*, even though 'brother' probably knew Leela had never got around to fixing the broken latch on her door.

Despite this lapse Leela thought a great deal about her safety. She carried a piece of glass. She carried a plastic whistle she had, to date, used only to toot her favourite song, *Tujhe dekha to yeh jaana sanam*. And she fretted constantly about being blackmailed.

Who are you afraid of? I once asked.

'People will take advantage of an alone girl,' she insisted.

Leela hid postcards she received from 'friends' who worked in dance bars in Dubai; postcards of places like Wild Wadi and Jumeirah Beach and Safa Park, places it pleased her to doubt her 'friends' had seen for themselves. 'Whores in fancy places. Huh!'

She ripped takeaway bills and tore or burnt with her lighter anything that could identify her by her real name or address.

She possessed no photographs of herself or anyone else.

She had one cellphone but three SIM cards, and the extras

she secreted in odd places—inside a shoe, at the bottom of a jar of dried red chillies, the stems of which she poked into her teeth, sometimes absentmindedly, at other times with a purposeful desire to clean.

And she wouldn't trust anyone with the bare necessities placed haphazardly around her flat. Leela had inherited a Godrej steel cupboard from a friend who had married a wealthy customer Leela jealously said was too old to piss without help. The cupboard overflowed with clothes—twenty-five pairs of jeans, half a dozen belts, enough t-shirts to stock a small shop.

She slept on a threadbare mattress, watched an LG television, assessed herself in a full-length mirror. She had a cooler; an old, overstuffed Kelvinator fridge, its surface plastered with stickers given free with her favourite cumin-flavoured biscuits, chocolate and toothpaste.

Leela also collected Ganesh idols, and she loved each of the dozens she owned like a little girl loves her Barbies. But she didn't love them enough to keep them clean.

I once walked in on a customer flicking at them with his kerchief.

'Achoo!' he explained, apologetically.

Now Leela murmured into her customer's ear, '*Jan-oooo*, wake up, *jan-oooo*.' He slept on. She raised her voice, '"Hensum"! Ai, hensum!'

The customer, who was not handsome, turned towards her and exhaled full-throatedly. '*Saala chutiya*!' cried Leela, leaping out of bed. Fucking cunt!

Leela's customer stank of vodka-chicken-onion-chilli-lemon and clearly he was no hi-fi-super-*badiya*-tiptop type. He had no upbringing.

'Dinner means drinks,' Leela agreed. She wrapped her slippery hair into an elegant bun and stuck in it a greasy spoon she found under the bed.

But this *maderchod*, motherfucker, seduced her into drinking so much she'd passed out and given him sex for free.

How had he done that, what did he say?

'"We'll go shopping," he said to me,' recounted Leela. '"Make a list, Leela meri *jaan*! *Sone ki angoothi*? Write it down! Silk *ki* nightie? Write, write! No, wait, write two-two silk nighties *andar ke kapde* matching-matching. The new Nokia that will go so well with your red handbag? Write that too!" And I fell for it! So busy I was making lists, drinking drinks, dreaming dreams of all the goodies fatso would buy for me, I forgot myself! And for what?' She motioned towards the customer, thin-lipped with distaste. 'This *khatara* pair of shoes?'

'Zero "kalass"!' Leela murmured to herself in the American accent she'd acquired watching MTV. 'Total *bakwas*.' Full of crap.

She made bad choices, Leela admitted, reaching for the Gold Flake she had secreted in the pocket of the customer's boxers.

Although she earned so many thousands every night she didn't know where to put the money, Leela was time and again seduced by the promise of more. And she loved not paying for her pleasures. After the dance bar closed for the night, Leela would waltz from table to table helping herself to half-smoked cigarettes. She would press her cherry-red lips to abandoned beer bottles. That the men whose leftovers she consumed with such relish had thrown all their money on her was an irony not wasted on Leela. It made the beer taste 'tight', fresh. Leela didn't believe this money should place her above such behaviour. On the contrary, she was transparent in her freebie-glee, failing entirely to notice how her curious behaviour was commented on by the other bar dancers. 'Not only does she put her lips on our boss,' they sneered, 'she puts her lips on those who boss our boss!'

Even the dancers weren't safe around Leela. Her kleptomania may have been an open joke in Night Lovers, but it was a joke taken seriously. If Leela asked to borrow a lipstick she might be told, '*Accha*, Rosy said first. After her, okay?' And then Rosy would dilly-dally before lying with *filmi dramabaazi*, '*Arre*, I *toh* forgot! Pinky wanted to do touch-up. One minute!' and so on until Leela's interest wandered and with it she too wandered out of the make-up room, to the great relief of her colleagues who had over the years forfeited compacts of the palest powder they stroked optimistically across their bronze cheeks and breasts, and hairpins washed with gold and sets of mirrored *choodis* to Leela's elegant if slippery-as-ghee fingers.

Leela didn't 'borrow' for profit; her intention was not to cause distress. Kleptomania was simply a part of her personality, an act as unconscious as the shake of her hips when a song played.

Leela also felt she was owed for having been taken advantage of when she was vulnerable. She might never get back at those motherfuckers. But everyone else was fair game.

'I'm a bar dancer,' she would shrug. 'Men want to spend on me. I let them.'

Leela encouraged her customers to buy her presents not just on her birthday, which they never seemed to notice occurred twelve times a year, but every time they met.

The other girls played the birthday game too and they conned customers into treating them and their children and their children's friends to 'burger-fry' and made-to-order cakes frosted with flowers. They sighed about how lonely the days were, how hard it was to remain faithful and if only one could watch serials, in particular the ones starring Tulsi, Prerna and Ba—'they were family!'—how quickly time would pass, and how quickly too might pass the temptation to stray.

Such words, if repeated often enough, might result in the gift of a TV, perhaps even a mini fridge stocked with silver-foil *mithai* rich with ghee and thick with nuts, or of a new wardrobe, everything within 'matching-matching' and sequinned one hundred per cent, so at night in the light of the creamy street bulbs, the bar dancer walking from her flat to an auto-rickshaw would cause strolling couples and children playing cricket between cars to stare, for she would appear like she was draped in diamonds sparkling so bright they could only be living, breathing things.

But Leela had no interest in merely big gestures.

Her motto was '"Kustomer" is Cunt.'

She didn't often have sex with a customer and when she did, perhaps once every few months, it was for money. Leela required payment upfront (five thousand rupees for 'one time' of intercourse)—and this was non-refundable if she developed cramps and had to excuse herself.

But even when Leela knew she would be paid, her customer was expected to suffer a trial period of humiliation before she would accede to him. He had to plead for her attention by phoning her dozens of times, by throwing money at her as she danced. He had to offer daily tokens—lipstick, earrings and perfume—through the security guard who stood outside Night Lovers, a giant of a man whose fiery red turban matched his temper.

And he had to run her errands. A customer entering Leela's flat, twenty litres of Bisleri water hoisted on his back, could be mistaken for a delivery boy.

Leela had so little faith in the ability of men to remain loyal and persevere that even 'husband' wasn't absolved from her itch to take advantage of the immediate. She would phone Shetty as he was driving over: '"Durrling", stop by Apna Bazaar na?' She would coo for rice and lentils, spinach and potatoes, for brinjals and beans that more often than not rotted in her Kelvinator in the same flimsy pink and white plastic bags in which they had entered her home. They rotted because they were never used: Leela refused to cook.

Like the models in the L'Oréal hoardings, Leela wanted men to know she was 'worth it'. But at nineteen, she was also aware that with girls like her opportunity didn't always knock twice. So she squeezed the men in her life like they were lemons and once she was through, she discarded them like rinds.

But every privilege has a price tag, and sometimes for money, and at other times because she had taken so much even she could not say 'no', Leela had to perform *galat kaam*, have sex with strangers in exchange for what she had convinced herself she had got for free.

ᥐ

Although they all did it, no bar dancer ever admitted to galat kaam. The only answer to a question around it was, '*Main mar jaongi magar* galat kaam *nahin karungi.*' I'll die before I perform galat kaam. The brazen one who admitted to it, it was said of her, was a *randi*, whore, and you could openly say to her in a voice as loud as you pleased—even though you were as guilty as she—'then you're a shameless liar you are, saying you're a bar dancer. You're no *barwali*! You're a waiter! A waiter in a Silent Bar and if you deny it your mother will rise from her grave and steal your booty from you. What's left of it, that is!'

A 'Silent Bar' or a 'Free Bar', as some referred to it, was often mistaken for a dive—it was poky, dark and loud and smelt strongly of incense, chutneys and tandoori meat. But in a Silent Bar men ordered food and drink so they could also order one of the 'waiters', as the women serving them were called, to give them a hand job. The waiters were almost always alcoholics or addicts. They tucked plastic bottles of cough syrup in the waistbands of their saris. They married men who would tear off and sell sewer covers in their desperation for brown sugar cash.

'A woman in a silent bar is no less than a *vaishya*,' Leela told me. 'And like all whores, she gets no respect because she deserves no respect. She wafts like a ghost, her face concealed by shadows, her voice never heard. Only her hands are of interest to anyone and these she must use until they erupt with sores.'

A Silent Bar was for destitute prostitutes, explained Leela, and in the hierarchy of the Bombay street, these women were to be pitied as much as the floating sex workers who sold themselves just about anywhere they could stand. Above them were the women in brothels who shared with their madam a fearsome relationship of slave to mistress. Above the brothel girls were the call girls who boasted, 'I graduated from Mithibai!'; 'I did English at Xavier's!' Who insisted, 'I'm from a good family that has fallen on hard times.' During particularly hard times, a call girl would slip into the lycra bikini she'd bought from Lokhandwala and custom-fitted with safety pins, she'd slip on her imitation D&G shades and, having slipped past security because she looked like she belonged, she would lounge by the pool of a five-star hotel and wait to be picked up. A call girl was no better off than a massage parlour girl whose pimp advertised her on the flyers he stuck on telephone poles, flyers that read 'Thailand Best Bod Massage Total Relex Please Call 98201*****'. Such a girl would work out of the string of 'beauty salons' that huddled behind the Taj hotel, and she was arrested so often, generally on a tip-off from a competitor, that she kept an overnight bag by the door to take with her to the police station.

But all of these women ranked below Bombay's bar dancers, and this was partly because selling sex wasn't a bar dancer's primary occupation and because when she did sell sex she did so quietly and most often under her own covers.

And so Leela, seeing no similarities between the bar and the brothel, convinced herself that she had earned the right to sneer at such women, and she did, with primness and pride, even though every one of them, like her, had been hurt and exploited, and often, if not always, she sold sex because she felt she had to.

When some people saw Leela they saw a *dhandewali*, working girl. But when she saw herself—in the mirror that hung behind her bedroom door or in the mirrored wall that was the highlight of Night Lovers—she saw a bar dancer. And the difference to her was the difference, she said, between the blessing that was my life and the blight that was hers.

∾

Turning her gaze away from her customer, Leela looked at me, her Gold Flake still unlit between her fingers: 'Light?'

I was happy to oblige, getting up from where I'd been sitting cross-legged against the Godrej, inside of which was a hollowed out copy of the *Hanuman Chalisa* stuffed with Leela's daily collection—the tips she earned for dancing.

The kitchen adjoined the Indian-style latrine and there was a box of matches amidst the tottering piles of dirty dishes—the debris of the previous night's mistakes. I looked around for some water to drink, but the Bisleri canister was empty and when I opened Leela's fridge I had to shut it quickly: it was a potpourri of rotting vegetables, the vegetable-gifts she so craved, which symbolized something to her—success, perhaps security—but which she never could find use for.

Opposite the kitchen counter was the only window in Leela's flat. Sunlight streamed in and brought with it the sounds of the street—the buzz, the barks, the drill-like honking. I leaned over and out of the window and ran my eyes over what was now a familiar view.

To the west, Mira Road shimmered with acres of salt pans, flat and blindingly white. Hundreds of minimum wage migrants, having left their families behind in Bihar and Gujarat, lived in tents they had pitched alongside the pans. Opposite the salt pans were residential buildings, their walls squeezed into one another like commuters on the Virar fast train. In these buildings lived 'everyday' people and here too lived some who elicited curiosity—Nigerians and Ghanaians about whom the local police would complain, 'They destroy their passports as soon as they arrive in India and then use their relationships with bar girls to manage the money they earn from net fraud and drug peddling.' The Nepali girls who lived in Mira Road in large groups in attic-sized sublets introduced themselves as Manipuris fleeing militancy. This protected them from prying neighbours who might discover they were illegal and for no reason other than *maska-mari*, to make themselves look good, squeal to the police—the overseers of Mira Road.

The police took *hafta-wasooli*, cash handouts, from people they knew could afford it—builders and cable TV operators, dance bar owners and bar dancers. And from those who could not but whose existence begged punishment—drug addicts and sex workers and the hand-clapping, sari-lifting hijras who would say to a policeman be he good to them or bad, 'Were you sent by the devil to create ashes from our lives?'

A policeman could grab Leela and with the force of his legs and *lathi* propel her into an auto-rickshaw. 'Paisa *nikal kutiya*,' he might say, calling her a bitch, demanding hafta for not arresting her. 'Arresting me for what?' she might have asked the first time. 'For being a randi,' he would have replied. He could steal her money, rip off her gold chains and slap her around.

Leela paid the police, because everyone she knew paid them too. And she was afraid. The police, she said, were quick with their lathi and leather belt, they had access to electric wires and a cattle prod, and they used these instruments without hesitation.

Even a handful of the middle-aged, middle-class Maharashtrian women who lived in Mira Road paid the police. But they did so because they were in business. They waited for their husbands to leave for work, and once they were gone opened their doors to the local pimp and to his girls. As the housewife went on with her life, as she cooked and cleaned, swept and swabbed, her husband's house would ebb and flow with visitors. At 5.45 p.m. the housewife would accept a slim wad of notes from the pimp, who moved quickly, pushing along his girls. She would then prepare for the return of her husband—set water for tea, fix a tray of snacks, refresh her lipstick. The housewife called this 'chai-*paani ka* paisa'. Pin money.

The street below Leela's flat was crammed with fruit and vegetable stalls, video game parlours and liquor stores. An apprentice cook rolled chapattis on the pavement outside the local 'hotil', a videotape salesman drew and coloured pictures he'd stick on to the covers of his pirated wares, a teenager in shades pushed a handcart of CDs past Paresh's Digital Photo Lab within whose walls Paresh Photowala was king, commanding 'Mouth wash *karo*! *Baal theek karo*! Right leg little front! Turn your body *thoda* forward! Smile! Smile! Smile *karo* yaar! Okay, nice, done!'

Then came along the strangest sadhu I had ever seen—a gnome of a man in purple tights, a purple puffer jacket and a knee-length orange robe. He bellowed, '*Shani ke naam*,' in the name of Shani, to the jingle of his flask of coins and in doing so encouraged the crowded street to empty miraculously before him.

Paanwala Shyam angled his brilliant white moustache to the sun, as though he knew he was being watched. He saw me and I waved down at him.

Shyam Kumar dealt in *supari*, of the kind used in paan, and it was whispered he also dealt in 'supari', codename for contract killing, for the D Company—the underworld organization headed by Dawood Ibrahim, the global terrorist.

Next to Paanwala Shyam, his paan stall and phone booth, sat Leela's tailor friend Aftab. Aftab worked under a sign he'd painted himself, it read 'Taylor All Tipe Alltration'. (To be fair to Aftab, his immediate neighbour was a 'Key Meker'.) Every few months Aftab designed and stitched clothes worth thousands for Leela's dance bar routine. The two would deliberate on the Yash Raj Films' style of the moment—'Cap sleeve, sleeveless, puff? Sharara pants, georgette sari, flared lehenga?' They would haggle over lace, beads and crystals; if they had to, they would shame the other into getting their way with the garment.

'You must have eaten *rohu* today,' Aftab would mock Leela through glasses shiny as sequins. 'You're behaving as tight-fisted as a Bengali.'

'You must have had to fuck one of your wives last night,' Leela would smile over her gold-rimmed aviators. 'You're in a mood blacker than a Bengali's arsehole.'

2

'Manohar wanted me to start modelling; he said I was bootiful'

Only bar dancers lived in Leela's building. They lived openly, their doors wide open, they lived in sixes—six teens or teen-faced twenty somethings, six Bedias, Chamars, Nats; six Shias, Sunnis, Kalbeliyas. Six squeezed into a 1 BHK, living in such disarray to a stranger's eyes it would appear they moved in the previous night. Six sprawled on mattresses that had, with time, been whittled down to a bony hardness, flat as the ground itself. Six had not a piece of linen between them. Six headrests were dupattas; dupattas were sometimes bed sheets. Six stuck their collection in their bras, their jewellery into shoes, their shoes and clothes into plastic bags.

They gave the impression that any time now they would pick up and leave.

Although their way of living suggested poverty, the bar dancers in Leela's building were not poor. They were certainly not 'Bombay' poor, which implied the meanest existence in a ramshackle chawl in which home for a multi-generational family so large they slept four, even five, to a bed, was an all-purpose *kholi*, ten feet by ten feet. Nor were they 'Indian' poor—whatever their past, their present claimed no acquaintance with the poverty of slum life; a pavement dwelling no wider than the tattered sari it was shaped from, the branches of the closest tree serving as a hanger for clothes, its nooks a rack for utensils, toys, a toothbrush.

On the contrary, Leela and her neighbours returned home

with hundreds, sometimes thousands, of rupees every night and they paid as much as ten thousand rupees in *bhada*, rent. Money was easy come, easy go, and some bar dancers treated it as such. They bought as many as fifty packets of gutka a day; gutka killed the appetite and kept them slim. They drank beer, beer kept them enthusiastic. And they loved takeaway, ordering, almost daily, biryanis or kebabs. Leela bought clothes she wouldn't wear twice, shoes she flung impatiently out of sight after a single use, and when she met someone she thought pretty she never hesitated to ask what brand of make-up they wore and then bought it for herself, never mind the price.

Partly because she spent so much, but also because she didn't know how, Leela made no investments. 'Banks require identity proof,' she said. 'Only God knows who I am,' she grumbled, meaning she had no paperwork at all.

Leela was paid in cash and she paid in cash too because her landlord was a gangster. Without a rent receipt she couldn't prove her resident status and receive a PAN card or ration card or open a bank account.

But the bulk of Leela's money, and that of every bar dancer, was spent on family members—parents and siblings and siblings' spouses and children. And so the first thing Leela did at the start of every month was send a cut of her money home.

'Secure the land,' she would call down the phone. 'Start building an extension to the house.'

'Look after the girls,' she would say of her nieces.

'Send them to school.'

'Don't send them to me!'

Home for a bar dancer like Leela could be Bombay itself—it could be Kamatipura or nearby Foras and Falkland roads, famous for selling sex.

Home could be Sangli, an agricultural district near Bombay that witnessed the highest number of farmers' suicides in western Maharashtra due to farm-related debts. A bar dancer from Sangli might be the daughter of a dhoti-topi-clad farmer forced to sell his land due to a single insufficient rain, left with no option but to allow his child to seek work in the big city.

Home could be the industrial cities of Lucknow and Agra up north, where the *khandani* families who traced their lineage to the courtesans had once thrived. Their historical patronage—the royals, the land-owning zamindars and briefly the British—had died out, leaving them marooned. For families such as these dancing for money was 'izzat *ki* roti'. Respectability. It signalled independence and upward mobility. Parents would exhibit 4×6s of their daughters singing and dancing in bars with enthusiasm and pride, giving these photographs greater prominence than even the sepia portraits of their revered ancestors.

Girls from other khandani communities like the Kanjar, Nat and Kalbeliya were often inducted into the profession at ages as young as six or seven—into street theatre known as tamasha in Maharashtra, into travelling groups of gymnasts, acrobats and trick-rope performers, into sex with long-distance truckers; in the lean season earning so little they could barely afford a sheet of plastic bags to separate their bodies from the highway.

Around the 1970s, bars in Bombay began to employ young women irrespective of their experience. This was for a new innovation called 'waiter service'. Waiters, in this context, referred to female servers. These women wore saris, not uniforms, and they were paid a monthly salary and did not have to survive on a collection. They were entirely different from the waiters who would go on to work in Silent Bars. Another innovation, 'orchestra service', referred to a live musical performance with a female lead. Bars then took a cue from Hindi films and the 'item numbers' gaining popularity—these were dance songs featuring starlets in plunging necklines and were conceptualized to sexualize a film without doing so overtly. Bars paid young women to dance to popular item numbers of the time and when this became their primary attraction they began to identify themselves as 'dance bars'.

Their success was evident in their growing numbers. In 1984, there were just twenty-four registered dance bars in the state. Ten years later, there were more than 200. And by 2005, this number had climbed to 1,500.

For women not mired in sex work, bar dancing offered lucrative advantages over other kinds of low-grade employment. In 2005, a bar dancer in a mid-level bar like Night Lovers brought home in one night what a cleaning woman or *bai* earned in a month.

More often than not, however, this new profession attracted girls like Leela—poor, barely educated runaways low on options. With its promise of immediate financial independence, bar dancing was a refuge from the horror of family life a young woman had no power to affect except by leaving.

◌◍

Still, for all these advantages, Bombay was unforgiving. It could be toxic, no less than an open wound. Naivety was fair prey and beauty unguarded deserved what it got. In a barwali's neighbourhood it was said, 'A "fresh piece" isn't secure from a boy child.'

To prove her point, Leela introduced me to her friend Anita. Like many bar dancers, Anita used only her first name with those outside the line, to protect her identity.

Anita had been raped by her father. But that wasn't '*aaj ki taaza* khabar'. Breaking news. She had had two sons by two different men. Or was it four different men? she said, with some confusion of how these things work. As she thrust and twirled to buy her sons milk and toys and to educate them in an English-medium school, she dreamt of when they would one day get 'big-big jobs' and say to her grandly, 'Now you put your feet up Mummy and let your daughters-in-law do everything.' But then her elder son, Sridhar, turned sixteen and one monsoon night he said to Anita in a voice as flat as water undisturbed: '*Khat pe chal.*' Get on the bed.

'I ignored him,' Anita said. 'Our chawl had flooded and the water had risen to our knees. Even my Reliance stopped working. So I thought to myself, "Poor boy, water is swimming in his brain. He's having a fit!"'

But Sridhar wasn't having a fit and the night after he didn't bother with the politeness of a request. He raped his mother. The night after that he raped her once more and when it was over and he had returned to his own bed in his own dark corner, Anita slid under her chunni and, gently patting her cheek, comforted herself, 'At least he didn't hit me. I'm an ugly face in a glamour line and had he damaged me further I would have been thrown out of the dance bar and forced to become a waiter in a Silent Bar. The humiliation! Merciful God, you saved me.'

Later, Anita would become what her friends called 'poetic'. On slow Monday nights when they took it easy in the make-up room, playing on the communal Sony music system not the item numbers they danced to each evening but the music they loved— old-time film songs like *Waqt ne kiya* and *Chaudvin ka chaand* and *Inhi logon ne*; songs whose lyrics they knew by heart, lyrics that would make them sigh—Anita and her friends would sit on the floor, each with a quarter of RC whisky by her side, and talk of things they could not to those outside their line. They would share old stories like they were sharing food; of how they had been forced into the line, of how the line had saved them from marriage to a friend their father owed money to; and they would share news, of a child who loved school, or a lover whose illness had spread to the mouth causing his gums to splinter and bleed—'punishment perhaps for loving a barwali'.

But Anita always took it too far, they said. She never could draw the line between sharing and simply 'being bore'. For no sooner had the quarter gone to her head, brightening her eyes and reddening her face, she would start to recite that old psalm, and with tears, lament as though she hadn't so many times before: 'The evening of the rains God cried. And with him, I cried too.'

Her tears were forced, dismissed her friends. 'Tears,' they would sneer, 'are the indulgences of those who haven't suffered enough.'

To avoid experiences like Anita's, the bar dancers in Leela's building refused to allow men to live with them. One might come across a child too young to understand what his mother did—who believed his mother and all of her friends worked in an 'ohfice', or that she taught 'two-plus-two' in a school far away. I might pass a man on the stairs, pressing his finger down hard on a doorbell, pressing his forehead against a door, but he would be a hotil boy delivering dinner or a manager desperate to cajole the *shaan*, the glory of his dance bar, to please return to work, he was sorry he'd called her a *chalu chamak challo*, a *rapchak*, a fast one, behind her back. 'Arre, he was only kidding, no?'

Men were chutiyas, Leela dismissed, making a fucking sign with her fist. They lived to profit from the women in their lives. Anita was no exception. I could do a survey with that little notebook-pencil of mine if I didn't believe her. It would reveal that every one of the bar dancers in Leela's building had either been sold by a blood relative or raped by one.

She knew one girl forced to take the virginity of all three of her first cousins. The other cousins had videotaped her.

These demons weren't prologue.

࿐

In the world of the dance bar, a mother could be convinced to rent her daughter out for twenty-five hundred rupees and something irresponsibly enticing—a TV perhaps, the first six months of cable paid for. She was petty and tight-fisted and had she any teeth they were orange—she was addicted to gutka and her favourite brand was the pungent Goa 1000, which she carried compulsively in her bra, in the waistband of her sari petticoat, or held in her hand, handkerchief-style. Mother drank on the sly and given half a chance would poach her daughter's customers. Not for sex, for conversation. She was that 'krack' from loneliness.

If mother wanted better for her daughter, and if she couldn't save her from the dance bar, she would find ways to compensate: she would cook hotil-style *khana* for her—mutton swimming in ghee, Chicken Chinese Punjabi style, buttery aloo-parathas dripping with fresh *malai*. She would order Guru Beer or a bottle of Old Monk rum, and she would ready all of this food and drink stylishly on a tray, intending to hover eagerly over her daughter when her daughter returned home from work, cajoling her to eat, drink, fatten up. But if her daughter returned with the dawn, then mother would put aside the tray, turn the cooler up high and, heating almond oil in a miniature *kadai*, massage the bruised soles of her little girl's feet. She would kiss her toes, calloused and hard with stamping thud-thud to draw from the *ghungroos* knotted around her ankles a sound sweet and inviting, and sing softly to her baby girl her favourite lullaby:

Go to sleep, princess, go to sleep.

Go to sleep, my precious one.

Sleep and see sweet dreams, in the dream see your beloved fly to Roopnagar and be surrounded by the maidens.

The king will garland you and—

Here she would kiss her daughter—

Kiss you on the forehead.

She would whisper: 'With a daughter like you only a fool would regret not having borne a son.'

If opportunity soured and galat kaam was inevitable, mother would spare her daughter the shame of being a *raste*-side dhande-wali forced to round up her own customers. She would have a quiet chat with the local paanwala and with the auto-rickshaw and taxi drivers who never said no to a money deal, especially on peak summer days when work was slow and hot winds struck a driver's face like a million slaps.

Some of these men were, in fact, pimps with a taxi or an auto-rickshaw at their service. They would listen for coded phrases like 'college girl' or 'back drive' or try to elicit interest in these matters by murmuring 'full service?' Some of them had been brought into the business as children—their mothers were sex workers for whom they pimped once they came of age. But they were not the only ones benefiting from the want of others. In Bombay city, it was whispered, for a certain kind of man born into a certain kind of life, only two things guaranteed money. Sex. And supari.

Mother would promise men such as these a fifty-rupee commission on every customer. 'Tell your catch I offer a discount on festivals,' she'd encourage. 'And 25 per cent off the hour if he breaks night with my child. I'll throw in dinner. Tell him that.'

'Dinner!' the men would snigger amongst themselves. 'Why dinner? Isn't your girl a feast in herself?'

But whatever mother did, and by God she did some shameless things, it was, I knew, almost always because she wasn't permitted, by virtue of her sex and class or her status as a financial dependant, to have a say in the things that mattered.

Fathers on the other hand had no excuse.

And yet, they were always Manohars—variations of the man Leela had been born to.

ᐁ

Manohar worked odd jobs in the military cantonment in Meerut, in Uttar Pradesh. He and Apsara, who had worked as a housemaid until recently, had Leela in 1986. She was their youngest and followed three boys. Apsara and her children were united in their fear of Manohar, who was an alcoholic and, from what I gathered, schizophrenic. For a time, Apsara suffered the most. There was the forced sex in front of the children. The stripping. One night Manohar tore off Apsara's Patiala suit—a voluminous item of clothing that covered her arms, stomach and legs—and kicked her out of the house. She crouched in the darkness until Leela was able to sneak out with a towel.

'We'd hear our mother being beaten and wouldn't know what to do,' Leela said. 'We had one of those old-fashioned irons; do you know the kind you heat with hot coals? I would heat it and start ironing all the clothes in our house. I didn't care whether they were dirty or clean, ironed or creased. Until the screaming stopped, until mother stopped sounding like a goat under the butcher's knife, I ironed.'

The cantonment was familiar with Manohar's temper. Apsara cleaned an officer's house. He pitied her, of course he did. But it was none of his bijniss.

'We had a lot of family around. My uncle, a cook, lived next door; my father's sisters lived close by. But there was no unity in our family. No response.'

For Apsara's suffering to end, Leela's had to begin.

And it did, when her daughter entered puberty.

'Manohar wanted me to start modelling, because he thought I was bootiful. So one day he brought home a video camera to make videos, for big-big Bollywood directors, he said. He asked me to take off my clothes. I was a child, remember, but I was smart. Not like my mother, dense as *seviyan*! I thought, "These are for bad films, blue-type films." So I said, "No. No, Manohar, I don't want to be an actress." He said nothing. Some days passed. One evening he came home and again he said to me, "Let's make a film." Again I said "no", confident-like. "Okay," he replied, "but if you don't act in my film the police will arrest you for being a disobedient daughter and push you into lock-up." I started to cry. "Is he lying?" I asked my mother. What could she say? "Don't be a stupid girl, stupid girl!" she said. "Do as he says!" That evening a policeman came home just like my father had threatened. He took me to the lock-up. I was terrified. So terrified I started doing *su-su* in my knicker. But the policeman didn't put me in jail. He raped me. His friend raped me. When they were done they said, "*Ghar* chal." Next month same thing. Again next month, and then the month after, regular as schoolwork. What did Manohar do? He called me a bad girl. "Bad girl!" he said. "I wanted you to be a model and an actress but look at you bringing shame on us." But he was smiling a joker smile. Manohar made sure I visited the police regularly and soon they came to know me well. Some of them were good to me—when they were done they would give me chai or a Marie "biscoot". They would say, "Tata! Bye-bye!" And they would make winking faces at me—as though I was a child!'

One afternoon when she was thirteen and visiting a friend—'I had only one friend and she was slow. I guess that's why she was my friend!'—Leela caught her reflection in a full-length mirror. It was the first full-length mirror she had ever looked into. For the first time in her life Leela saw herself not just in her entirety, but as an individual, an entity. It was a startling feeling and it revealed to her things she had never before seen.

She was scrawny, yes. But at five feet two she was already taller than her mother. Tougher than her mother. And she was sharper than her brothers, all of whom had played hooky through school. The twenty-year-old used his fingers to count three pigeons nibbling grain. The one in the middle had a leg shorter than the other and used his disability as an excuse for petty perversions: he would take advantage of the rush and confusion of students leaving the local school to feel up girls under the starched chunnis they draped protectively over their indigo kameezes. He would pick the boys' kurta pockets for coins, sweets, ballpoint pens.

With the suddenness of a shove, Leela realized she was better than everyone around her. With adult-like clarity, she knew she could do better.

But if she wanted change, she would have to seek it for herself.

'By then the girls in my school knew what I did and when I

passed by they would hide behind their hands and whisper, "Leela is dirty, don't talk to her."

'So I thought, "Why should I spoil my name? If I'm forced to do *ganda* kaam, I should do it where no one knows me. Otherwise, what chance will I have in life? And why should I feed my father with my money? I do the kaam and he gets the *inam*! Arre *wah*!"'

Leela stepped away from the mirror.

A few days later she stole money from her father's pants pocket for a train ticket to Bombay. An older woman she knew from around town had moved there and begun working in a dance bar called Night Lovers. She agreed to introduce Leela to the owner.

He was a God-fearing man, the woman said to Leela on the phone from Bombay. He was the father of two children, so no *ladkibaazi* for him, don't take tension. He was a south Indian Shetty, first name Purshottam.

∾

Someone warned Leela, 'Mira Road "tation"!' and so she knew where to get off, even though what she knew she momentarily forgot when she saw before her Bombay.

'So big!' she gasped with wonder, descending on to the platform with her shabby little suitcase. 'Too, too big!'

Unsure of what to do, Leela did nothing, and that was a misstep she was not likely to repeat. She was elbowed and shoved and her breasts were squeezed like oranges for juice by half a dozen hands. She would have fallen off the platform and on to the tracks if she hadn't grabbed on to a coolie hurrying past.

Bombay was crowded, Leela concluded as she dusted her salwar kameez off with what was to become her trademark equanimity. And it wasn't anything like a Bollywood film, she admitted to herself with a sigh. She took another look to be 'double-sure'.

Where were the white mountains, the shiny red *gaadis*, the yellow-haired *firangs*?

Which way was Marine Drive, where did Amitabh Bachchan live, and was it true this was a city where women drank side by side with men and men wore shoes crafted from the skin of cows fattened on 'Lundun's' greenest grass? ('Accha where was Lundun? What do they wear there?')

And yes, Bombay smelt. Not in the manner of the Meerut cantonment with its profusion of giant, flowering neem trees, their branches shooting out like the fingers of a ravenous *dayan*, witch. Back home, when a woman stepped out of her house and into the courtyard to dry her freshly washed hair, the breeze carried with it the scent of Chandrika soap and Amla Shikakai. And when a father was clever enough to marry his daughter off well, the air scooped into its arms the aroma of the finest vegetarian delicacies and of garlands of marigolds and *gajras* of jasmine.

Not like that at all!

Bombay smelt of shit. And everywhere she looked, from the train tracks, where people were strolling like they were in a park, even laying clothes out to dry, to the hillock that sloped into the opposite side of the tracks, between the neatly plotted lines of the spinach and potatoes someone enterprising was growing, all Leela saw was shit.

How her eyes smarted!

And that *tatti* smell combined with all the other station smells—of sugarcane juice and *vada-pav*, fresh fruit and flowers, fish spiced and fried, and of the hot, steamy fragrance of milk being poured into a giant utensil of freshly brewed masala tea—made her giddy.

In the midst of these thoughts, Leela was accosted by a woman who enquired in a kindly tone if she was lost and on hearing her story, commiserated. 'Let me walk with you, *beti*,' she said. 'Of course, I know where Night Lovers is, so famous it is, and only ten minutes away. No, don't argue! You are like my daughter only.'

But despite the woman's familiar appearance—her coin-sized gold hoops, the umbrella sticking out of her shiny pleather bag— she was, Leela would soon discover, a brothel madam who pumped her business with runaways from the 'chiller room'—children's homes run by the government's child welfare wing.

She took Leela to her brothel. It was a kholi, crowded, filthy and shrill with the sounds of a baby's cries. Under threat of scarring Leela's face with acid that she stored in a baby feeder, the madam forced Leela to have sex with several customers. Four days later, striped with bruises, Leela jumped out of a window and escaped. She eventually found her way to Night Lovers.

Leela was not surprised by what had happened to her. She was relieved.

'Had that bitch not caught me, a policeman would have,' she said. 'And he would have stuck me in the chiller room in Mankhurd. Do you know what they say about that place? That it's a brothel for Bombay's *mantri log*, politicians. The police act as pimps. Why? *Kyunki* police *ko sirf* paisa *chahiye*. The police only want money. They round up orphans and runaway girls and then call the mantri *log*, "Please sirji, sahibji, come *na*, pick and choose." The mantri *log* fuck the little girls and afterwards tip the manageress, "Thank you so much madam." They are men, and that's what men do. But she's a *harami* danger-*log*! A bitch, a dangerous one. She's supposed to be a mother to the girls, but during the day she makes them weave baskets and at night she cracks apart their thighs with a lathi!

'What luck I got saved!'

It wasn't mere luck, it was written, and that's why Leela was unperturbed by the startling welcome Bombay had given her. It was the start of a new life as *jyotishji* had described it when he read her palm just before she fled Meerut. Even though it was understood he was meant to lie and prophesy only a peaceful marriage and a fertile womb, he couldn't help himself. '*Kathin*,' he had mumbled through a mouthful of paan, juice slip-sliding out as he spoke. 'It will always be kathin.' Difficult.

Leela had smiled at jyotishji, even tipped him an *ek sau*, a one hundred. At thirteen she had the self-awareness to see and to accept the truth.

And the truth was this—she was no virgin, not even in the way some girls had sex with their first couple of boyfriends and when dissatisfied with the results, shrugged the young men off as mistakes and pronounced themselves pure. She didn't come from a good family: her father didn't have the upbringing to beat her mother behind closed doors and then, too, only after he'd gagged her mouth with his hand. Even his daughter's bijniss he couldn't keep quiet about, *gaandu*-maderchod. Wasn't it true everyone in the cantonment knew how Singh had upgraded to a twenty-six-inch TV? Fucking *chutmaar*!

And the truth was that although she wanted to better herself she wouldn't always be up to the task.

She was just a girl. No match for destiny.

In any case, she knew this too—you didn't fight destiny like destiny was your mother and you could win. Destiny, Leela knew, like she thought she knew who she was, was an unbreakable promise. An infallible prayer.

She embraced it.

Leela had worked at Night Lovers ever since and she never did return to Meerut. She warned Apsara: 'If you give Manohar a paisa of the money I have earned, I will come to Meerut and pry out every one of your teeth.' Even Apsara, who many in the cantonment believed was mentally challenged, could understand that her daughter might harbour ill feelings towards Manohar. She took Leela's threat seriously and until the time she could cash them in hid her daughter's money orders in her underwear.

Manohar believed Leela's whereabouts were unknown to his family. He tried to file a Missing Persons report with the police, but they were after all the same men he had rented Leela out to. Believing he was temporarily hiding his daughter, as a way to increase their lust and extract more money, they paid him no heed.

'Your little whore did not go to school alone,' one of them informed him.

3

'A bar dancer's game is to rob, to fool a kustomer'

I met Leela six years after she had left home, those six years later she was only nineteen. Unlike many of the nineteen-year-olds in Mira Road—still studying and still living with their parents— Leela had a job, had bills, had sex. Her confidence in the sexually charged environment of the dance bar confused me. She was surrounded by men night after night and these weren't just any men, they were often drunk and aggressively lustful. I asked Leela how she did it and shrugging she said, 'Otherwise?' She meant she had no option.

But she thought about my question and she answered, not that night, or the night after, but later. 'When you look at my life,' she taught me, 'don't look at it beside yours. Look at it beside the life of my mother and her mother and my sisters-in-law who have to take permission to walk down the road. If my mother talks to a man who isn't her son, brother or cousin, she will hear the sound of my father's hand across her face, feel his fists against her breasts. But you've seen me with men? If I don't want to talk I say, "Get lost *oye!*" And they do. And if I want a gift or feel like "nonwedge" I just have to tell them and they give me what I want, no questions. They thank *me*. Every life has its benefits. I make money and money gives me something my mother never had. *Azaadi*. Freedom. And if I have to dance for men so I can have it, okay then, I will dance for men.'

And so Leela chose azaadi, and she chose also to curtail

it, by defining the parameters of her life as the area from her flat to Night Lovers, a place whose rhythm and cadences she lived by. Anything outside these self-imposed boundaries, even if it was an adjoining suburb, she firmly referred to as 'Bombay', as though Bombay was elsewhere and distantly so. Bombay was also *bahar gaon*, out of the village, abroad. 'I'm going abroad,' she would tell me and I would gently rib her saying, would you like a lift to the airport? 'I'm going abroad,' she would say to me, and in her wistfulness she revealed her hidden yearning. Leela knew what it meant to go abroad, and for all her talk of freedom, she didn't always believe she enjoyed it.

Leela reached Night Lovers before the other dancers because she wanted to help Shetty. But she was also determined to make her presence felt. *Maar-peet* or *nakabandi*, gangvar or encounters—he would always be around. 'God willing,' so would she. To show she wasn't one of them she referred to Shetty not as seth, boss, as they did, but PS. She snitched on those who poked fun of his 'pregnant' belly or his 'outing problem'.

Leela explained this 'outing problem' to me: 'He pushes and pushes and pushes,' she whispered, concern writhing on her face. 'But nothing comes out! So what can he do poor durrling? Of course he has to put his fingers in! Take it out himself! But it's so stubborn, it takes so long, once he's done he just runs out, no flush, nothing. I've told him a hundred times, "How can you greet kustomers with that hand? Run it over my face even? And don't you slap my buttocks!"'

'I want to take him to medical,' said Leela. 'But if his outing problem stops, his wife will wonder how and then she will find out about me.'

How would she know? I asked curiously.

'Sometimes,' Leela reddened, 'he soils his pants. If we fix him, he says, his Mrs won't have any pants to clean.'

About an hour after Leela arrived, around 3 p.m. that is, Shetty would send off a fleet of auto-rickshaws to pick up his *heeremoti,* jewels—the bar dancers so skilled their dancing paid for his 'electric-paani'.

If one of them phoned to whine about her bruised knee or aching back, he would cajole and calm her and immediately send her the spotless white van he kept on standby. Inside, the dancer would find a box of her favourite mithai, a bouquet of flowers and more often than not, attached to a stem with the tender fragility of a love letter, a rolled up five hundred rupee note.

'My *chokris* are high maintenance,' boasted Shetty.

'Some are quite fair-skinned,' he added, as though in explanation. 'Not fair like a heroine! But more fair than kustomers. And they have to be kept happy. If I don't treat them well, they will run off. And if I lose my best girls, I'll lose my biggest collections. So any time one of them does *nautanki,* I throw notes at her. No worries then! Why no worries then? Because money is music. Yes or no? Yes! One note, two note, three note, four note . . . and they dance like it's a *sone ki barsaat!*' A shower of gold.

The bar dancers arrived in groups of three, even five, for they shared auto-rickshaws and taxis and with them came the fragrance of Jovan Musk and Revlon Charlie, and if they'd recently been sent to Dubai or had lovers who'd been there, of Armani and Versace. Because they were freshly bathed their hair was wet, combed through and tightly pulled back, and perhaps their skin glowed beneath all that make-up. The chiffon of their saris and the sequins of their lehenga-cholis created a dazzling, blinding effect and when they stood before the altar it appeared as though they had gathered not in prayer, but in celebration.

The altar wasn't easy to spot, but it was there, above the cash register. It held a gold-plated statue of Lakshmi, a string of chillies and lemons to protect against evil and a diamond-studded statue of Ganesh. As the bar dancers prayed, Shetty sang a short hymn. Then sniffing hungrily at the incense he said, *'Bhagwan ka* naam *lo aur* kaam *shuru karo*!' Take God's name and start work.

Once in a while Shetty would clap his hands and in loud imitation of the ringmaster of Gemini circus—which he visited every time it came to town—command, 'Now, brothers and sisters, *kahin mat jaiye,* seat *pe rahiye, kyunki aap dekhnewale hain*—' Don't go anywhere, stay in your seats, because you are about to see . . . in the time I knew him, he never once completed this sentence.

I asked if it was because he'd forgotten what came next.

'Of course not!' exclaimed Shetty, taken aback. 'But suspense is good, yes or no? These girls of mine never go anywhere. What Gemini-shemini, most of them don't know what a joker is! So the suspense factor, it is important. It can be useful. Say one night one of my girls decides she wants to leave for another dance bar, say the manager there has promised her a bigger cut of her collection. But as she's leaving she may think, "Arre, but what were we going to see?" Who knows, maybe this curiosity, the superstition that she doesn't know what she was meant to see, will encourage her to apply the brakes. Maybe it will keep her close to me.'

'Do you watch thriller films?' Shetty asked, noticing I was unimpressed. 'You never know the truth until the end, am I right? Right! And a gambler? Does he know whether he's going to win or lose? Does he? But still he picks up the cards! My girls are gamblers, it's the nature of their job, understand that. They gamble with their health, their safety, their good name. All I'm doing, really, is offering them something worth gambling for.'

Shetty treated his bar dancers like children. He teased, humoured and manipulated them. If he yelled at them one day, he would bestow great affection on them the next. And although he had a fierce temper, they rarely saw it. He had beaten one of his dancers in public, only once. He conveyed disapproval with a smile, so they were never sure whether he was being serious or silly. To be safe, they assumed muscle in his voice and almost always did as told.

෨

Of course, Shetty's successful management of Night Lovers hinged on more than his relationship with his bar dancers. They were, in fact, the least of his concerns. How he dealt with the police, the local bureaucracy—the Brihanmumbai Municipal Corporation (BMC)—and with the criminals who came calling for their cut of his profits was crucial to his survival.

Shetty didn't just pay hafta, he ran favours, wrote off tabs, even offered women if the women consented and they always did because it was expected of them.

Shetty used the term 'politics' to explain why he paid hafta. It connoted a sly corruption, but one he was compelled to feed for his survival. 'It's police-*log ka* politics,' he said to me, '"bureaucracy" *ka* politics.'

The police said that not all of them took hafta, and they were right. They argued that only those who broke the law felt compelled to pay hafta. They were wrong. Hafta was like salary. You forked over a mutually acceptable amount every month, negotiated a raise every year and in return received a service. It was a culture upheld in the police station itself, where some senior inspectors demanded hafta from their subordinates. This in turn led their subordinates to demand hafta from the people who lived on and off the street.

Bar owners who resisted payment, which could vary from five thousand rupees to a crore of rupees every month, depending on their income, suffered immediate consequences. Laws like the Bombay Police Act and the Immoral Traffic (Prevention) Act, which clamped down on sex work, were most often used against dance bars. They were nebulous because they dealt with the arguably indefinable subject of morality. They could be applied to whomever the police saw fit. If they chose to, the police could arrest Shetty for obscenity—by deeming even a fully clothed girl obscene—and have his licences revoked. He would then, once more, have to pay a string of BMC officials large bribes. Back in business, if he still refused to pay the police, the situation would merely repeat itself.

So Shetty paid hafta and he also paid a builder to construct a concealed room at the back of Night Lovers. This was how he received the service he paid for: when the police were compelled to conduct a raid, which could end in the arrest of members of Shetty's staff, who would then be liable for release only after posting bail, one of them would forewarn Shetty via code—often a predetermined, humorous text message about wives and girlfriends. When Shetty received the text he would either send his bar dancers home, or hustle all but a couple of them into the secret room thirty minutes before the time designated for the raid. When the police arrived they would find the lights on, the music low and a few waiters serving snacks. They would find it hard to concoct charges for arrest.

'See how I protect my kustomers,' said Shetty self-righteously. 'If I didn't pay the police they would snatch up not only my girls, but my kustomers. Give them slappings; threaten to tell their wives, shove them in lock-up.'

Sometimes the police *were* customers. When a policeman entered a dance bar, he might declare, 'This is my area.' This was how he would tell a man like Shetty, as if Shetty didn't already know, that he was from the local police station and could make a nuisance of himself. So there was no question of giving him a bill. He was offered cigarettes and whisky, kebabs and paan, even stacks of ten rupee notes to throw on the bar dancers.

Or, if the local police station required a new set of furniture—chairs, tables, lights, you name it—the senior inspector might send his men over to Shetty's to 'borrow' whatever it was they wanted. It went without saying that the borrowed items were never returned.

Shetty preferred the police to the BMC—less red tape. But

he had a soft spot for another band of extortionists—the criminal gangs of the underworld he had to pay to leave him alone.

The relationship between dance bars and gangs went a long way back. It is generally accepted that organized crime in Bombay developed from the needs of Prohibition. When Prohibition was relaxed in the 1960s and 'permit rooms', as they were called, for a permit was required to buy and drink liquor, became popular, the owners of these permit rooms began to face demands from the gangs that had prospered and grown powerful from bootlegging. If they didn't pay up they were physically attacked; their customers were harassed. When permit rooms converted into dance bars and proved a success, the demands of the gangs grew. They wanted not only more money, but to own the dance bars either in part or full. Their involvement, as with all businesses they were connected with, brought greater political scrutiny to the dance bars, leading to higher licensing fees, and from the police and BMC, created demands for more hafta.

Shetty, who had inherited his father's Udupi restaurant, described himself as a self-made man. He had, after all, turned the restaurant into a profitable and very popular dance bar. He was impressed by gangsters, he said, because they too were self-made. Their bold subversiveness was so extremely masculine, it represented to him the freedom ideal. Even small-time gangsters, the only kind of gangsters Shetty would ever meet, carried arms and delivered threats. When they came by Night Lovers to pick up their fee he treated them like favoured customers. Although he paid them twenty thousand rupees a month, and much more on Diwali and the New Year, he liked to add a tip to the envelope he handed over. He gave them drinks on the house. He took them to the make-up room to meet his prettiest bar dancers. He'd hang around them like an enthusiastic teenager hoping to pick up gossip about celebrity gangsters—Dawood, Abu Salem and Chhota Shakeel.

You should ask Dawood for a job, I once joked, having just

watched him escort a couple of thuggish-looking, gold-wearing, poorly-concealed-pistol-toting men to the door.

Shetty's eyes lit up and then, just as quickly, dimmed. 'But I'm a family man,' he sighed.

༄

Night Lovers began to fill up at about 7 p.m., when most customers made their way from their place of work to the dance bar. Although their persuasions varied, the clerks and career alcoholics, tradesmen and twenty somethings who walked in were of modest status, expectations and income. They knew to go only where they were welcome. In a dance bar, their money could buy the attention of a beautiful woman. And unlike a high-end South Bombay nightclub, it was democratic. There was no entry fee, no sartorial standard, no pressure.

I guess it had what some might call glamour. The women were responsible for this, of course, but so too was the decor, which brought to mind a set from a 1970s item number, resplendent with kitsch and glitz. Night Lovers had golden pillars and out of each pillar jutted a Medusian head. One wall was of glass, the table legs were disco balls and opposite the altar hung a full-length painting of a naked woman, her modesty protected only by the length and lushness of her blue-and-pink hair. Although Shetty's style was to me unique, in the context of the dance bar it fulfilled expectations. Night Lovers was designed to enhance its disconnect with the world outside its doors—the real world, that is.

Leela danced alongside about twenty other girls on a slightly elevated stage in the middle of the bar. For the first few hours she was enthusiastic, for she was drunk and had dragged on an accommodating waiter's joint. She feigned pleasure, winking naughtily at the customers, pouting at their glassy-eyed reflections in the mirrored wall behind her. And she was careful not to miss a single step of the dance routines she practised so diligently at home. That was what she was tipped for after all—to beguile like an Aishwarya, a Sushmita, a Priyanka.

Do what you want, Shetty instructed his girls, but give kustomer-sahib *paisa wasool*. The customers should get their money's worth.

Leela wasn't allowed to speak with customers during her performance and she rarely did. In fact, she noticed only those who threw money on her, as was the custom, or asked the steward standing by for this purpose to place a garland of hundred or five hundred rupee notes around her neck. If she was feeling wicked, she would accept the money and staring deep into a customer's eyes, silently mouth: 'Is this all you think I'm worth?' She would rub her eyes and pout, murmuring, '*Hai! Kyun na main sweecide karoon? Kyun na main apna sar ohven mein daloon?*' Why shouldn't I commit suicide? Why shouldn't I stick my head into an oven?

If the customer was familiar with Leela's ways, which, truth be told, were the ways of all experienced bar dancers, he'd swat her away with a good-natured laugh.

Not so a fresh one. 'No!' such a man would cry, rummaging frantically through his wallet for more money, even if it was his last few notes, seeming to really believe Leela would kill herself right there on the dance floor. Leela would acknowledge the fluttering notes with a smile and for a few seconds, perhaps even a minute, dance as though the customer was the only man in the room. But even before he could settle back to enjoy her attentions, Leela and her unspoken promises would have glided towards another man.

In a Bombay dance bar it was not just money that was power. Nakhra was power too, the power to break a fresh one's heart.

Soon, however, Leela's intoxication, her playful moments of spinning around the dance floor, would evaporate. She felt as she always did towards herself, her job, her life—used, wasted, bored.

Her customers were hardly hi-fi in their cheap, choppy bowl

cuts. Their shoes were much too large as though they expected—at their age!—to grow. The *chhotu*-types wore heels and when they smacked their feet on the table tops like Raja Hindustanis, Leela was faced with rows of potato holes. She swore she smelt feet, despite the strong cologne her customers reeked of, and when I asked of the smell, she said 'dirt'.

They were predictable too in the way they started out polite, calling her 'Miss' to her face (if '*pataka*' and 'item' when she turned) and how only a whisky-Coke later, they were indistinguishable from roadside Romeos—those open-shirted, *deshi*-drinking thugs who made caressing gestures with their hands as they muttered filthy words to passing women.

Customers pretended it was the alcohol making them so, when the truth was they didn't need an excuse to hiss at her breasts, 'Ai booty, what's your loveline number?'

She disdained their amateurish attempts to get her attention. How one would say, 'Here, take my bijniss card,' as a ruse to hold her hand, even though he knew well that touching a dancer inside the bar wasn't allowed. How another thought a hundred and a compliment about her 'white-white' complexion would get her to linger.

When they were real drunk, they were real cunts. They would rate the girls aloud, shouting rudely, 'Five on ten!' 'Eight on ten!'

There was always one who would attempt to dance and that was so 'no kalass'—the girls didn't care if he was a '*zabardast* paisewala', had plenty of money, or a '*dus* paisewala', had none—they would mouth *gaandu*, arsehole, to his face. They would hoot when the bouncer dragged him off the floor.

⁓

Leela dismissed young men her own age. They were strugglers, she knew, with little control over their lives. Their mothers and wives kept a steady grip on their earnings and monitored their social lives to protect them from women exactly like her. They were, at best, good for flattery and a few tens. They were dreamers too and they dreamt of things Leela had no interest in—of working in an AC office, of upgrading from a motorcycle to a 'motor-gaadi', of going on pilgrimage to Tirupati.

Many young men flush with hundreds and excited to spend it all were, typically, new recruits in local gangs. They were boys really, who had gone from being useless and unemployable to becoming 'men', paid regularly for their allegiance and muscle. Few had known temptation and as they faced it now, they didn't quite know how to respond. Their first taste of dance bars would come courtesy of a senior gangster, a Bada Don, for gangs routinely used places like Night Lovers to impress future recruits.

'See all of this,' the Bada Don would say gesturing grandly, the gold chains around his neck gleaming brightly. 'All this can be yours to enjoy if you have the money. But how will you earn so much money, my young friend? Tell me? Think! That's right! It will happen if you work for me.'

This lot was under no illusion. They expected to die young or live behind bars and boasted a heady recklessness Leela found profitable, but distasteful. Playing games may have been part of her job, but life itself, she knew well, was no game.

But the worst customer barring none was the *'chhota mota sindhi chamar chor'*. This peculiar dance bar phrase amalgamated the qualities a bar dancer considered most undesirable. These included being stingy and of low caste—sometimes as 'low' as that of the girls themselves. A chamar chor was a misguided young man, most often in his late teens or early twenties. He robbed things shiny and expensive-looking from his parents' home and sold these to his friends or the petty thieves they knew, for what was known as 'cheating *ka* paisa', small fraud money. He'd snatch cellphones laid casually on shop counters. Racing past on a stolen motorcycle he'd tear purses from the arms of women in auto-rickshaws.

The only place a chamar chor could enjoy his money without coming under suspicion was in a dance bar—even though a bar dancer like Leela, knowing well the source of his largesse was no more than a fistful of *jhol*, stolen goods, would accept his notes with a grimace.

Bar owners like Shetty encouraged men like the chamar chor. They were fair game. Shetty enjoyed playing games. Unlike Leela, he was sure of winning.

He would welcome the chamar chor with fanfare. 'Consider this your home,' he would say, pulling the chamar chor into an embrace. 'Think of me as your father. Fathers and sons don't count money between them, do they now?'

Once the chamar chor ran out of money, he ran up a debt, siphoning Officer's Choice and 8 p.m. down his throat, demanding garlands of notes. As soon as he got drunk he became a real cunt. Typically, he would take over the dance floor, offering his best imitation of Amitabh Bachchan in that most raucous of Bollywood songs, *Jumma chumma de de*.

'Chumma!' he would scream, begging for a kiss.

'Chumma!' he would lunge across the floor, sliding this way and that.

'Chumma!' he would sigh and soon enough, with a 'chumma', collapse.

And that was the beginning of the end of his simple life.

For when the chamar chor's debt touched a comfortably round and suitably large figure, say one lakh rupees—an amount, given the temptations, he could spend within a week—Shetty would move in. He would tell the chamar chor to pay up, or else. That the chamar chor couldn't was a given. So there were two ways he could resolve the problem he had created. He could go to jail—which implied not just a meeting with a magistrate but beatings courtesy an accommodating policeman. If he was vegetarian, finding chicken skin in his food, if he was non-vegetarian, discovering worms. Or he could do Shetty a favour. The favour might involve six months of washing dishes in the kitchen, or running errands—ferrying the dancers back and forth at all times of night and day. But if the chamar chor was unlucky, he would suffer what men like Shetty called a 'Bombay Special' and the only response to a command involving those words was 'Yes sethji'.

A Bombay Special was Bombay; it was everything the name evoked: shock and awe, expectation, desperation and always the underlying question, 'Why me?'

A bar owner says, 'I need someone shot. Here's the gun. Now scram, cunt.'

The chamar chor replies, 'But . . . but I don't know how to fire a gun!'

The bar owner responds, 'Ai, taking part in a competition? Want to win first prize? Arre, hold the gun two inches against the head and pull the trigger. *Ekdum khallas*. Smooth as butter.'

Then he laughs, 'Why the fear, my friend? Afraid of firecrackers?'

And so it was that a young, silly, petty thief would come to kill for a bar owner with a gun, a grudge and a penchant for gangster films whose script he claimed as his own.

So it was that a killer was born.

If the chamar chor completed his Bombay Special there was no way back. If he did not, there was no way out.

But if his success was no fluke, if he could go on to shoot another and one more, he could perhaps one day become a Bada Don.

A Bada Don was a gangster without regrets. He was a man like Feroze Konkani, a Dawood man, now dead, once the city's highest paid shooter who by the age of twenty was said to have been involved in eighteen killings. Dawood rewarded Konkani with a flat in upscale Juhu, a car and pillow cases of cash he lavished on bar dancers.

His women would have known that Konkani's money, like that of all Bada Dons, was 'haram *ki kamayi*', unclean and immorally obtained. It was '*dadagiri ke* paise', acquired through extortion. They didn't care. They didn't care because in their business honesty was no virtue—it only equalled greater poverty.

And poverty eventually made criminals of everyone, even those who swore to resist—it was the only way to transcend the free fall of their marginalized lives. So everyone was a 'history-sheeter', a person with a record of committing crimes, and it was considered better to be with a successful thug, a Bada Don, than with a chamar chor who depended on his woman even for his evening paan.

A bar dancer who found herself dancing regularly for a Bada Don and then one night having with him 'filmi sex'—sex practices he insisted she copy from pornographic films—would quell any second thoughts she might have on the matter, by repeating to herself, as though in doing so it became true: 'Men are all gangsters anyway. So why shouldn't I throw in my lot with a successful one?'

She would reassure herself, ticking off the fingers of her left hand as she spoke aloud to anyone who would listen: 'Gangsters have money. They're smart-looking. They have *tashan*, style. What's not to like? And they're straight talkers. "Fuck me," they say, straight off. They don't suck your blood, *choos choos ke*, *choos choos ke*, like other men do. And even if they are trouble-makers, they aren't trouble that lasts long. Here today, dead in a police encounter or a gangvar tomorrow. A Bada Don knows death is his shadow. He understands that the life he has chosen can be so rich, so fulfilling, bursting with pleasure and with pain, because it is also so brief. So today means everything. Today my gangster will feed me and drink with me and we will go driving in his Honda City to Aksa beach and behind the bushes we will lie down, and afterwards, when we are done, we will have chai and samosas, and if not him, then at least I will pretend we are husband-wife.'

Leela said, 'A few girls do get scared once they discover their man is a murderer, a don. They stop meeting him, change their cell number, change even the dance bar where they work. But what does he care? As long as he has money to spend, he will find women to spend it on. We are all the same to him. The living same-same, the dead same-same. But sure, there are others who will only go out with gangsters. They find it thrilling! The first time a chamar chor kills a man he sees his life flash before him. He goes home, says goodbye to his family, locks his bedroom door and waits for the police. But do the police care if some *do take ka* bhonsdi ka lund, two-bit cock of a whore, was shot in the head while pissing on the wall of the JW Marriott? Days pass; days without money. What does the chamar chor do? He goes back to that same dance bar. He begs the bar owner to find work for him, any work will do, he says, making his meaning clear. And so he kills again. But this time the killing doesn't scare him. It's a thrill, a powerful thrill, because he killed a man and suffered no retribution; because for a few seconds of work he made more money than his father has ever brought home, forget in one month, in six months, and his father is fifty years old and still has payments left on his two-wheeler. And it's a thrill because he knows that the only thing that stands between him and money is his conscience. He can make money for the rest of his life because in Bombay city if there is one thing you are never short of it is people. He thinks to himself, so easy! "Trigger *daba*, figure *kama*!" And this power, this freedom, this is what attracts a bar dancer to a killer. Do you know why? Because we yearn to be free.'

ॐ

Of course, a true Bada Don like Dawood wouldn't visit a Bombay dance bar, or a dance bar in public. But a Bombay don was no Dawood and neither was the average Bombay man. And of all the customers from all over India Leela would perform for at Night Lovers, no one was more vulnerable, or to use her word, 'pathetic', than the middle-aged Bombay man.

'Give him a chance to say two words,' grumbled Leela. 'Two! He'll say two hundred.' As evening's shadows lengthened, so would the stories—the unhappy marriage, the wife who might as well have padlocked her knicker-bra, the children who flip-pantly nicknamed him Mr ATM.

Leela may have found her customers pathetic, but they made me sad. For a few, visiting a dance bar was no more than a boys' night out. But others were clear, even humble, in their loneliness. I knew this not because these men hit on Leela—not all of them did and many took their time doing so—but because of their consistent, often futile attempts to get her to talk to them, to listen to them and to remember them when they returned.

Bombay has a torrential number of people. There are people everywhere, and they are confined not just to public spaces and the interactions of push, shove and pull but to what should be personal spaces. For want of space children sleep with parents, for greater want parents sleep in the doorway of their homes. Husbands and sons heft their bedding down the street, unfurling it on the floor of their local temple or mosque.

In its death, privacy takes with it intimacy. And so when men in situations like these seek intimacy elsewhere, one of the first places they go to, because it is socially and economically acces-sible to them, is the dance bar.

But Leela didn't see nuance. She didn't have to.

What are they like? I asked of her customers.

She shrugged.

What do you know of them?

'My head,' she said, tapping her temple, 'is not a computer. I have no place for *altu-faltu* info.'

Perhaps because Leela enjoyed B-grade horror flicks, she remembered the ones with the terrible features. Those she hoped wouldn't return. The gangster with the cauliflower ear, the construction worker with the forest of hennaed knuckle hair. That Parsi fellow with a hole in his tooth so large Leela swore she'd once seen him pour a quarter into his mouth only to have it come tumbling out.

To Leela a customer was a 'Ramzan goat'. Destined for

slaughter. And she, Leela said to me, must wield the knife that would slit his throat, cut his head off and hang his carcass to drip, drip, drip. Never forget, she instructed, a bar dancer's game is '*lootna*', 'kustomer *ko bewakuf banana*'. To rob, to fool a customer. And every bar dancer prayed for the sort of client whose indulgence would make newspaper headlines. A scamster like Abdul Karim Telgi, who was rumoured to have lavished around ninety lakh rupees on a bar dancer. Or Aman Mishra, a young man who became famous for spending over twenty lakh rupees on a bar dancer he was infatuated with. (Two years later, after he was revealed to be a conman, Mishra kidnapped the bar dancer for ransom.)

Although Leela had yet to be discovered by an Abdul or an Aman, she was undeterred, rarely allowing her distaste for her current (what she considered lowly) crop of customers to show. She was professional and she knew that sort of behaviour would get her fired, wife or no wife.

But of course, if Leela didn't know her customers, fewer knew Leela. They didn't even know what to call her, she was always calling herself something different. One night she was Kareena, having just watched the actress Kareena Kapoor in *Dev*. On another night, she would introduce herself as Rani, for Rani Mukherjee in *Yuva*.

ᴕ

When she was done with work, Leela would clean up in the make-up room, say her goodbyes and stop by Shetty's office for her money. All the money thrown at her was picked up by a steward and placed in a *dabba* with a single key Shetty kept in his wallet, which was, in turn, chained to the pocket of his front shirt. Shetty would open the box in front of Leela, note the amount in a dense, cloth-bound register and pay her cut accordingly. Leela could never be sure that everything she earned went into her dabba and not into that of another girl's by mistake or into Shetty's wallet on purpose. But she had no choice but to believe him, just like every bar dancer in Bombay believed her manager.

Tucking her money away in her bra, Leela would head to the back door to avoid bumping into customers. She'd pass through the kitchen, inevitably filthy at this time of night, through the alcohol-storage area with its imported whiskies and country liquors, even with packets of *haath bhatti*—home brew sold in plastic bags for a few rupees, and slip into the auto-rickshaw that had brought her to the dance bar.

Leela had known her auto driver Badal for several months; he was her protégé. They had met in Kamatipura when he was fifteen and his mother Bani's pimp. Leela saw her childhood self in Badal. She could see his adolescence was as much a zone of desperation as hers had been. When she wasn't engaged with customers Bani lavished her energies on Tommy, a pet goat with a rosy red collar she hoped to train for the circus. How quickly money ran out! Sometimes there was so much of it, Bani would order beer and biryani and suddenly all the building's 'whores', rendered shameless by hunger, would decide she was their best friend. They would eat until they burped and then Bani would order Badal out to buy paan so sweet it made the teeth squeak, and the women would chew and gossip and gamble away whatever little money they had left.

When the take was low, Bani encouraged her three-year-old daughter Baby to stick her head out of the window and help her and Badal outsell the competition.

'*Baby clap your hands!*
'*Smile!*
'*Happy smile,*
'*Big-big smile,*
'*Actress Kareena Kapoor-like smile!*
'*Now swish your dress to and fro,*
'*And smile, Baby smile!*'

Leela brought Badal to Mira Road with the hope that he could build a life for himself outside the brothel. If he drove a rented auto-rickshaw, in a few years he might earn enough to buy his own. One day perhaps, Leela daydreamed for the boy, he could graduate to chauffeuring a car. So she set him up with a madam down the road from her flat and in exchange for running errands and keeping watch over her girls—making sure they didn't run away, that is—the madam allowed Badal to live rent-free. To resolve the issue of a driving licence, since Badal was underage and looked it, Leela helped out with a modest loan which would serve as hafta and an introduction to the local constable's wife, a woman who had impressed Leela with her 'pull'.

Not only could she get things done through her husband, Leela said, but also through his boss, a senior inspector with whom she was conducting a passionate affair.

4

'My mother is fat. And very, very simple'

A few weeks after I walked in on Leela's customer, I walked in on her mother Apsara lounging with Leela on the bed, scratching at her scalp with a toothpick. 'Mummy, dekho meri friend!' Leela jumped up. She threw her arms around me and then stepping back pinched my cheeks like I was a little girl. Ouch! I cried. Leela laughed with pleasure. 'You delicate darling,' she said in English. 'You princess!'

Apsara stuck the toothpick down her kurta and beckoned to me. 'Come here, my daughter,' she squeaked through a mouthful of gutka. I grinned inwardly. Her voice *did* sound like a tape on fast forward. 'Let me look at you.'

I joined Apsara on the bed and without preamble she ran her hand over my face. 'Appearances are so important,' she said, pulling at my skin. 'More than the goodness of her nature,' she jammed a thick finger into my mouth, almost making me gag, 'it is the appearance of a woman that can decide her destiny.'

Apsara said, 'Smile!' and smiled as though to show me how. The few teeth she had were grimy with gutka stains, jagged like miniature peaks. She retrieved her finger and continued trawling the landscape of my face, stroking, pinching, prodding. Any time now I expected her to say I wasn't worth the price I was demanding.

'Where do you live, beti?' she asked.

I started to answer.

'Do you live alone?' she interrupted. 'And what does your *pitaji* do? And your mummy? You a Hindu, *na*? Where is your native place? You speak Hindi so well beti. And English also Leela was saying!'

Thank you, I replied.

'Where did you go to school beti, here or in bahar gaon? What is your job? How much do they pay you?'

I told her.

'So little!' Apsara gasped. 'Is it enough for you beti? What are your monthly expenses?'

Leela playfully slapped Apsara's cheek. Then she smiled at me as though to say, 'you're a good sport!'

Satisfied with her quality check—'Live well! Live long!'— Apsara spat into the palm of her hand and smoothed back my hair. 'Now beti,' she said, spraying gutka on my face, 'I'm going to tell what my favourite TV shows are. You tell if I chose right or if I chose wrong.'

The similarities between Leela and Apsara were so uncanny, I was charmed. Mother and daughter loved to talk, each exclusively about herself. In conversations with Leela if the subject somehow turned to me, Leela would tug at her hangnails in frustration. Was I there to learn about Leela or to be bore? Because if I was going to be bore . . . Leela's time was money, there were places she could be. PS had, in fact, just called to invite her for a meal at Pure Wedge, she would have me know.

But if I sidestepped the risk of being shown the door by conceding quickly and always, Apsara never did.

A conversation between mother and daughter, as I would soon discover, sounded like a peak-hour fight over a bus seat. Leela would snap, '*Saand!*' Buffalo! Poking a meaty finger into her daughter's narrow waist Apsara would snort, 'Huh, *marial!*' Sickly!

And yet, there was a grace inherent in their behaviour. Their hand gestures were as elegant as mudras—classical dance movements that amplify a point or emotion. It was a trait I had assumed Leela had picked up in the dance bar; but seeing her next to Apsara, their fingers in ballet, I realized that genes had something to do with it. Leela had Apsara's nose, she had her mother's laugh. It was as inviting as the open doors of Night Lovers on New Year's Eve.

೦෴

Apsara had moved in with Leela just the day before. She had, without warning her daughter, whom she hadn't seen in almost a year, taken a fast train from Meerut and walked in on Leela while Leela was asleep.

'*Mera to* heart attack *ho gaya*!' said Leela. I had a heart attack!

Apsara had brought with her several cartons of Meerut specialities including *gajak* and *rewri*. She had hoped these gifts, humble though they were and unworthy of her glamorous daughter, would distract Leela's attention from the two sizeable, rope-tied suitcases they had been crammed into, alongside clothes, utensils, photos in their frames and her favourite vase with its clutch of red plastic roses.

But Leela missed nothing. 'Such big-big suitcases!' she exclaimed. 'Only for two weeks?' That was the length of time Apsara usually visited for.

'Only if my daughter throws me out,' said Apsara. 'But if she doesn't,' she continued quick as can be, 'mummy will stay on to pamper her. To cook for her and wash her clothes; to do massage for her head and press her legs. To comb her hair one hundred times every night.'

Leela attempted to demur, 'You shouldn't leave your husband alone, mummy. You know that, you know why.'

'It's been so many months, Leela!'

'But you know what he's like, mummy!'

'Give me a chance, beti.'

And so Leela did, if only, as Apsara soon revealed, because Manohar had proved himself to be a *Rakshas* No. 1. He had broken one of her fingers, imagine it!

But he had done that before, Leela reasoned impassively.

Battered her so many times, their neighbours in the cantonment could only respond with a weary silence when Apsara insisted she was unable to judge distances and had, since she was a child, tripped down stairs as a matter of course.

So why leave now?

'I can't knit any more!' cried Apsara, throwing her large, fat hands in the air. Tears rolled down her face.

Pathetic, Leela mused. Manohar had pimped Leela, and Apsara had protected his shameful secrets as though they were her own. But God forbid someone mess with her knitting!

'I went to doctor sahib,' Apsara sobbed. 'But he said, "It's too late, Mrs Singh, you are too old. Nothing can be done to straighten this finger. Just manage best you can."'

'Why did he do it, Leela?' wailed Apsara. 'Knitting is my all! Didn't he know it? The years I spent by his side! And he couldn't see it?'

Now Apsara, caring little that we had only just met and if anyone's presence in her daughter's flat needed explanation it was mine, launched into her personal history. She put aside her knitting, which she clearly hadn't given up on despite the difficulties the task presented, and to ensure my full attention, hijacked my wrist. She moved this way and that, edging so close I could smell her gutka breath. I appreciated its minty freshness for it seemed she also enjoyed deep fried snacks.

'Every time my mister gets drunk,' Apsara said, breathing heavily, 'he behaves like a buffalo rampaging through a sugarcane field. With God's grace if I manage to run away all he can do is throw something in my direction—a chair, a stool, the knife he insists on keeping in his back pocket like he's some hunter-wala! But if he catches me—*Hai Ram!*—God says bye-bye and the devil says "Apsaraji, *kya haal chaal?*" One limb at least goes *ka-ra-ck!*'

Leela rolled her eyes. 'Apsara is fat! And she's very, very simple.'

By 'simple' Leela meant 'stupid', but in a kindly way.

'My mother is simple,' she would shrug, when I asked why her mother hadn't taken her away from Manohar. 'My mother is simple!' she would comfort herself, when she heard from her brothers that Apsara had spent her money orders on custom-fitted motorcycles and satellite radios for them. Leela's brothers were unemployed, and hoping to remain so, reminded her in STD calls she paid for that they were praying for her health.

'Buy yourself a box of Shimla apples,' they would instruct, as though it was on them.

'Eat almonds soaked overnight for breakfast.'

'Drink a quarter litre of cow's milk every morning.'

Leela saw through their solicitousness. 'What will happen to them if I fall ill and cannot dance?' She stuck her palm out. 'Madam, paisa *do na, do na* paisa madam.' Beggary.

All of this, Leela wanted me to know—Apsara's attitude towards her sons, her sons' stupidity and sloth, who knew, perhaps even Manohar's antagonism—was a product of Apsara's weight and girth and the fact that she was unforgivably simple.

Leela looked at her mother thoughtfully. 'Since I could see, I saw my father beating my mother. I didn't know A-B-C, but I knew what it meant when Manohar threw aside his plate. That's why I ran away. Because he abused her. Once he hit her so hard she fainted. And because she didn't say No, he abused me; and I knew that if I stayed on, if I didn't say No, one day he would do the same to my children. Now I see her sons have inherited this quality from their father—they think women were created by God to serve men like them. And that's what makes me so angry; that she can see what they think of her, she can see it because I can see it and neither of us is blind. And yet she supports them. She loves them. She loves them more than she loves me. But why? Why when I'm the successful one, the one who works, who feeds her, who clothes her, who asks if she has taken her medicine? Why when I'm the one who had the courage to leave for the city? When I'm the one who became a success and made money, makes money!

Money like a man! No, no, more than a man! I'll tell you why.
Because they're boys. And I'm a girl. Nothing but a girl. The
value of a boy is twice that of a girl—isn't it so mummy, even
if the boy is useless?'

Apsara's eyes welled. 'That's not true.'

'Yes. Yes, it is.'

'It's not true, Leela.'

'Okay.'

'I'm not strong like you.'

'You're not strong—that's true! But remember mummy, your
sons have wives now. You keep pampering them with my money
and so they like you. But what will happen to you if I stop
dancing? Will they hold you as close? What will happen, mummy,
when I decide that like them I don't want to work, I want to be
taken care of? One day mummy, I will want to be loved. What
will happen to you then?'

'Your brothers are good boys, Leela.'

'Don't empty your *thali* mummy, that's all I'm saying.'

'You're giving Soniaji the wrong impression about us,' cried
Apsara, throwing down her knitting needles in distress. 'What
will she think? Soniaji, Soniaji ours is a good family. From my
side at least we are of a good caste. All our women have either
been housewives or in service—cooking, cleaning *handi bartan,
vagera vagera*. No bar background. Not like some bar dancers
Leela knows whose grandmothers—grandmothers! spent their
life in Lucknow's *mujra* salons. *Chee, chee, chee*!'

And still Leela entered this line, I said.

'Yes,' Leela turned to Apsara wide-eyed. 'How did that
happen?'

'What can I say?' Apsara reddened, looking down at her
hands. They were thick with gold rings; presents from Leela.

'Leela was headstrong. She would make her own friends and
she had big-big "*Haathi Mere Saathi*" ears. She heard stories
about Bombay, of its dance bars, of how much money you could
earn. Imagine it! Money for *naach-gana*! Leela loved dancing,

did you know that? She won every dance competition ever held in school. She was known as *"Chhoti* Madhuri" after Madhuri Dixit. Accha, remember *Ek, do, teen?*'

'*Ek, do, teen,*' Apsara sang throatily, '*char, paanch, chhe, saat, aath, nau . . .*'

'Mummy!' Leela screamed, theatrically sticking her fingers into her ears. '*CHUP!*' Shut up!

'*Uff!* Okay, fine, I won't sing. Where was I? *Hahn,* so one day without telling anybody this girl here ran away!'

'Just like that?' said Leela, sounding intrigued. 'Just like that I ran away?'

Apsara ignored her.

'I ran away because I like to dance, is it?'

'I remember that morning very well even though it was how many years ago, four, five, hahn Leela?' Apsara picked up her knitting. She was gamely working on a pair of pink booties. 'Her father had left the house without making a show for the neighbours. What relief! What a change! You know, in those days I would serve him his morning cup of tea trembling. Trembling! Anything could go wrong. The sugar was too little or it was too much, the milk should have come from a cow not a goat, why is the plate white not blue, oh I can't tell you what a mad rakshas he was. Much worse than now! But that day he was quiet as a mouse. I looked up, "*Devi,* have you answered my prayers?" But, of course, no luck, and only the day after that he was as he'd always been, shoving me back to front, front to back like I was one of the cows papaji had given him in dowry. In any case that morning he behaved properly and so I went to Leela's room to tell her the good news. "Who knows," I was going to say, "maybe our luck has changed?" And I wanted to see her smile. Poor girl, the evening before Manohar did something too dirty. He had insisted on hand-feeding Leela and Leela never liked that sort of bijniss, she's a very headstrong thing. She spat out the food! Manohar gave her one tight *jhap* and shoved the food back into her mouth. What did Leela do?

She vomited—right into her plate! And then, oh well, you know what happened next for the love of God why are you making me repeat this story? This is not Ramanand Sagar's *Ramayana*! No need for repeat broadcast!'

Apsara gnawed through a grumpy pause. 'Anyway,' she continued, 'this girl here vomited and my mister shoved her face into her vomit and wouldn't let go until she ate everything, until she ate every bit of her own vomit. What was it now let me think? Bread-omelette, hahn Leela? Now I can't remember, but just you imagine it! Imagine eating that! How I suffered watching her, I couldn't move, I couldn't speak, I said to myself, "God, wouldn't it be best to fling your humble servant under a truck? That would be kinder, no?" But Leela's room was empty. Where was Leela? First I thought maybe she'd gone out to play. After all, remember beti, she was only a child then, in small-small *chaddis*, not even a woman.'

'My mother is very simple,' said Leela grimly. 'Play?' she glared at Apsara. 'Play? After Manohar started sending me to those maderchods who would play with me? Who would talk to me? "Dirty girl! Dirty girl! Dirty girl!" That's all I heard in Meerut mummy and you know it as well as I do—play, it seems! Someone has played a trick on you! Someone has snatched your brains!'

Apsara's bottom lip trembled. 'What do I know? I'm an illiterate village woman. Did I even see your father's face before I married him?'

'I told you one hundred times not to call him my father. He's a rakshas!'

'When his parents came to my parents' home,' Apsara turned to me, 'the first thing they asked for, even before they asked for tea, was to see my father's tractor. To check if it was good enough for their field. They even went into the kitchen to inspect our utensils, the cooking oil. My grandmother was cutting "wedgetables". They showed her no respect. They looked above her, at the spices. They looked behind her, at our kerosene stove.

They looked top to bottom, at the big-big pots in which we had stored our rice and dal and atta. But they didn't look at her. Later my mother-in-law, God bless her soul, she took me aside, to counsel me, I thought. What did she say? "After marriage if we discover you aren't a *kunwari* ladki, a virgin, jaan *ki kasam*," she said to me, "I will cut your breasts off with the same knife I use to cut the stems of the potato flowers and I will feed them, piece by meat piece to the crows.'"

Leela exhaled with frustration, 'Good story mummy.'

'Don't talk,' snapped Apsara. 'If I drop one stitch I'll have to start all over again.'

'Accha, you know Sheila?' she turned to me.

I shook my head.

'Our neighbour, that one who lives there?' she pointed abstractedly. 'Short little thing. Wears too big-big gold earrings. Face like a little boy's. No, wait, face like a rat! She's a rat face! Have you met her? Have you met rat face?' Apsara giggled gnomishly.

She had managed to move on to an entirely new topic. This too, I would learn, was a standard Apsara dodge.

'You don't know her?' she said, sounding frustrated. '*Ajeeb si* ladki *hai tu*. What an odd girl you are. Anyway, Sheila's third daughter—what did she eat to have three daughters?—she just had a baby. Another girl, imagine it! I said, "Okay, okay, don't take tension, I'll make clothes for her." That way at least they won't have to buy any. Everything is so expensive these days and babies don't stay small-small *na*? Now look at Leela, how big she is! When she was small do you think one banana would have satisfied her? Or one *cheeku*? Never! Everything had to be two-two, three-three. Banana two-two, cheeku two-two, even egg-fry two-two! What a healthy eater she was by God's grace!'

Apsara sniffed and wiped her face on her sleeve.

Leela rolled her eyes. 'Don't look so worried,' she said to me with a short laugh. 'Mama's simple, I told you. Next time for sure she'll ask if you know her mother—who died of tuberculosis before I was born. You just say, "Of course Apsaraji, her *kadhi chawal* is *mast!*"'

'I may be simple Leela,' snorted Apsara, 'but I'm not deaf.'

Leela nipped the knitting out of her mother's hand and threw it petulantly on the floor. 'Enough of this mummy,' she said in the baby voice she used to great effect with customers. 'Why are you always thinking about other people? Let the child run *nangapanga*, naked. You give me head massage!'

5

'I want a good break, yaar.
No cut-piece, sidey role for me'

Apsara was not the only woman in Leela's life. She was certainly not the most important. Beautiful Priya was. Leela loved her best friend Priya the way I imagined she would one day love her own child—with a longing even immediate proximity could somehow not fulfil. She petted her, fretted over her health, insisted on sharing everything with her—sleep, dreams, secrets. Clothes, meals, cigarettes.

If Leela could, she would have shared life's every experience with Priya.

Leela's friendship with Priya proved to her that she could love someone and in turn be loved, with no caveat on either side. Her love was so sincere, so pronounced, it was like she meant for it to say to the rest of us, 'this is how you should love me.' And also, 'why don't you love me like this?' In the world in which they lived, in which deceit equalled success and all success was ephemeral, Leela and Priya's friendship was the one true thing they could count on.

Leela also coveted what Priya had, but in a wistful way, entirely without malice.

Who could blame her?

Priya had sculpted cheekbones, a sharp nose, endless dancer's legs. She had 'rich girl's hair'—straight, slippery, shiny. Translucent skin. And unlike any bar dancer I knew, perfectly white teeth.

When we first met, I couldn't wrap my head around her. She wasn't supposed to be here, on Leela's bed, the mattress pinched thin and punched with holes, so long past its expiry date it should've been junked in the marsh that separated Mira Road from the rest of Bombay—children floated paper boats on it, scavenged plastic bags they would sell by the kilo from it, they called this bobbing of other people's faeces and filth *dariya*, the river. And she was certainly not supposed to be sitting opposite Apsara—forever chewing, spitting, knitting, grousing Apsara, whose idea of beauty was a plate of *bhajjias* or a new ball of wool.

Having introduced us, and making space for me on the bed, Leela drew Priya's head into her lap and started to gently comb her hair. Her face bright with adoration, she said to Priya, as I saw her do every time they met, 'Ai, *tu* star *kab banegi? Hame yahan se kab legi?*' When will you become a star? When will you take us away from here?

'Arre arre,' giggled Priya coquettishly, 'if I'd wanted to get into Bollywood wouldn't I have become a household name years ago? You know directors have been breaking my door since I was this big!' She pulled her hands apart to illustrate.

'But I want a good break, yaar. No cut-piece, sidey role for me. Shah Rukh, Shahid, Saif.' Her velvety lips parted. '*Koi* Kapoor, *koi* Khan. Should be of some level *na?*' She looked slyly over, to make sure I was listening. 'Otherwise, purpose?'

On an average day in Bombay thousands of men, women and children take acting and dance classes and make the rounds of studios hoping to catch the eye of the person who will transform them from the one who gazes awestruck at the big screen, to the star who looks down from it.

A couple of Old Monk rum and Cokes later, it all came out: 'After I got married, I gave up my Bollywood dreams,' admitted Priya. 'I wanted only to look after my husband, myself and our baby. I never went with kustomers or even visited friends, ask anyone! I have one vice, gutka. But then my baby died. My husband left. I was alone. What's an alone girl to do? Chase films? Chase fame? No! Drink! Why? Because a man will desert you, work will desert you, children will desert you, but swear on my mother, alcohol will never desert you.'

'Agreed,' said Leela. 'Bottle is your best friend.'

'But of course,' Priya yawned dismissively at me, her breath gutka-rum-Gold Flake, 'you won't understand any of this. You're an outsider. You know zero of the troubles I've been through.'

She eyed me expectantly.

I complied. Why don't you tell me?

Leela put aside the comb, unfurled herself from her lotus position and cuddled up to her mother, her expectant face turned to Priya. Priya's stories, as time would tell, were like a *saas-bahu* serial—they went on forever and became increasingly, grippingly complicated. Although the narration of her love stories allowed Priya to inhale most of the friendship oxygen, Leela didn't mind. It allowed her to admire her friend's astonishing beauty without embarrassment. 'When I take tension,' she said to me, 'I close my eyes and think of Priya.'

☙

Shortly before she turned eighteen—and of legal age—explained Priya to me, she married a man called Raj. They had become lovers a few weeks after he'd begun to visit her dance bar, Rassbery, which, like Night Lovers, was also in Mira Road.

'No, it wasn't too soon! Have you even seen Raj?' Priya's eyes gleamed. 'Oh you're missing something! He has Saif's tashan, Shah Rukh's muscles and Salman bhai's . . .'—here Priya winked suggestively and pulled her hands apart, wide, so I couldn't miss what she meant—'you know! "Priya, Raj! Priya, Raj! Priya, Raj!" Everywhere we went people would look at us and sigh, "Priya, Raj!" We were that first-class-looking together! I even had his "foto" on my cell! I lost ten good-good kustomers because of him, the kind that would throw one thousand rupee notes on me. Raj would come into the bar and I wouldn't look at anyone else. "Janu darling, my darling janu," I would whisper into his ear all evening.

Kustomers would yell, "Ai ladki! What's wrong with you? Am I paying you to talk to another man?" Oh you should have seen me snap! "You bastard pimp!" I'd yell back. "You're only a kustomer you are and that too you have a little-little dick I know it very well! But this one here,"' Priya's face softened, '"he's my husband! My life! My love!"'

When she discovered she was pregnant, Priya hired Pramila, an orphan who lived in the same chawl doing odd jobs, to help out at home.

'Raj said, "I beg to you, don't keep her here. I'll give you five hundred rupees, give it to her and pack her off." But did I listen? No! We fought and fought and we both got so hot when he slapped me I slapped him right back. He slapped me again and before he could do it one more time I stopped his hand like this and said, "Durrlings! She's a girls, I'm a girls. What can go wrong if we live together?"'

After she delivered a stillborn, Raj asked if she would mind if he slept with Pramila—to get over the trauma, you know.

Priya said damn right she would mind.

He went ahead anyway.

'I was so furious I got divorced that evening itself. Lucky me,' Priya said, as though she had demonstrated great foresight, 'we hadn't married in court.'

'That Pramila!' Leela narrowed her eyes. 'You loved her like a sister! If it wasn't for you . . .'

'Yes,' agreed Priya. 'I treated her like my best friend. But never mind her, didn't my Raj return?'

Leela nodded enthusiastically.

And did you take him back? I asked, on the edge of the bed.

Unless Priya was being creative, this was one of the most gripping, and bizarre, love stories I had ever heard. Romeo and Juliet had nothing on Raj and Priya.

'Just like that?' Priya scowled. 'Do I look like a Thane-side dhandewali? First, I flat refused. For one whole week every time he came home I'd grab my *dawai* and pour it down my throat.

What medicine? You name it. I bought it. How I scared him! The second week he brought me a hamper of chocolates and oranges. I snatched up a blade from my box, cut one of the oranges and I flung it at him, like it was Holi *ka gulal*! Then I cut myself, *kachak*! Here, see the mark,' she gestured proudly. 'The mark of my love! My anger!'

Apsara nodded appreciatively.

'The week after that, he took me to a hotil and we sat in the coffee shop. He spoke to me franks, decent. *Bade log ki badi baat*. The big talk of big people. He touched my hair. He fed me with his own hands, a sandwich. Then, only then, and not one minute before mind you, did I relent.'

For an outsider like me, Priya's anxious pursuit of love was difficult to comprehend. She was young. She made her own money. And she was a beautiful woman in a line in which beauty was prioritized and privileged.

And yet, Priya's beauty did not give her the upper hand in her relationships. Having won her over, Raj was again taking her for granted, by starting an affair with one of her colleagues at Rassbery. He was open about it, speaking of the woman and of her adoration for him like it was information Priya would benefit from.

'He's full enjoying!' Leela said indignantly.

Priya wanted the affair to end. The woman was a whore. One look from Raj and nine months later she would—for sure!—turn up with twins. So she planned to confront the woman that evening, to match fists if necessary.

Just in case violence introduced itself into the conversation— and Priya knew it would because 'that one' was 'no kalass'—she wanted to carry ammunition. Leela wilfully suggested a hammer. But Priya didn't have the stomach for a fight that might scar her face. She considered chilli powder, and on Apsara's insistence planned to stick a small but heavy torch into her handbag.

'If she acts smart give her one like this!' Apsara said, making a thwacking motion with her beefy fist.

'No,' Priya shook her head. 'I want to punish her, but in my own way. Oh her truth-lies, lies-truth, oh her whisperings into Raj's ear are driving me mad.'

'*Doglapan*!' cried Leela, curling her lips. Treachery!

What did she say? I asked.

'Priya? Which Priya? Oh, that one, true, she's a booty. But you know we call her mattress. What to do? So many men have slept on her!

'Are you the prime minister's first born that Priya will throw down a red carpet for you?

'Do you know, Priya has only two sets of clothes, and one of those she sleeps in? Be careful! Could well be her body is crawling with lice!'

'Imagine!' glowered Apsara. 'Imagine saying that about our Priya. Priya beti?'

'Hahn, aunty?'

'Beti, I'm telling you, hit her one hard on the head. That will silence her for good.'

'Yes,' encouraged Leela. 'Beat her! Beat her Priya; beat her repeatedly so that the next time she goes to work it's in a Silent Bar.'

Apsara started laughing like that was the funniest thing she'd ever heard. 'What a good idea! Make her a . . . a,' she giggled and hissed.

'A lundchoos!' she hooted. 'Make fatty into a lundchoos!' A cocksucker.

6

'To be held, even in the arms of a thief, is worth something'

Priya walked into Rassbery carrying in her handbag a torch and a sealed packet of chilli powder. She had no intention of using either. She should have been emboldened by her love for Raj, but she hoped, frankly, that Barbie had stayed home.

But Barbie (real name Panna Lal) sauntered right out of the make-up room. How had she known Priya had arrived?

She walked straight towards Priya.

Although Priya stood her ground, she couldn't but inwardly recoil. Barbie was taller, broader and meaner than anyone in Rassbery, man or woman. She was 'fair like a ghost', fat 'like a fisherwoman', and the belly chains she wore were thick as fingers.

What did it matter? Raj was bewitched. And so were Barbie's customers.

Their behaviour! Thumping tables, screaming out, jumping so their shirt buttons flew open and their Nokias fell out.

The noise! 'Wah! Wah! Wah! Barbie-Panna Lal! Wah! Arre wah!'

Barbie may have looked like a bai, but when the lights were turned down and the music was turned up, she blossomed like a lotus in a pond. She laughed with vigour and gyrated like all she wanted was you.

Priya knew the other dancers envied her beauty, but she knew too that they pitied her presumed naivety. What excuse did she, of all people, have to lose a 'husband', a baby and now a boyfriend? Look at Barbie, they marvelled. So single-minded, so sure of herself. Mark our words, the dancers said, Barbie's babies will carry their father's name as proudly as a constable wears his badge.

'You!' Barbie said, interrupting Priya's thoughts.

'Yes, so?' demanded Priya, sounding braver than she felt. 'Is this your father's house?'

Barbie considered. No, it wasn't.

She extracted a packet of gutka from her bra, ripped it open and emptied the contents into her mouth. 'Good you came,' she said, flinging aside the packet. 'We have matters to discuss. It's best you stay away from my man, let me tell you franks. Otherwise God knows what I may do. Ask anyone, when Barbie gets angry Kalyug descends.'

'Why would I come near your man?' asked Priya, amazed. 'Did I lose my mind on the Bombay-Poona highway? But you're right, we do have things to discuss. And what I have to say to you is this—stay away from *my* man, Raj. Stay far, far away. Like you don't know we want to marry, shameless whore! We want to, we will, and when we do, I won't have you storming the *pandal* making a first day first show for everyone.'

'Arre madam!' spat Barbie. 'Have you lost your mind? You come here!'

'Huh?'

'Arre, come here, I said! What are you afraid of? If I wanted to beat you, you sickly little twig, you think I would have waited this long? Come here, I said!'

Priya glided up defiantly. 'What is it?'

'See here!' Barbie thrust her wrist into Priya's face.

Priya didn't blink. Barbie's wrist had been gouged into.

Placing her bag down, Priya began to roll up her left sleeve. 'Do you think my hand slipped while I was cutting apples and oranges?' Her wrist was charred with cigarette burns.

Barbie touched Priya's wrist. 'So,' she said, unfurling a smile. She edged closer to Priya, until Priya could smell her sweet gutka breath, her sour, combative sweat. And Barbie could smell Priya too, Priya supposed—the Revlon Charlie perfume she favoured. They sniffed each other out like dogs assessing threat levels.

'Born yesterday?' Barbie said kindly. 'Think we're fighting over a vada-pav?'

She grabbed Priya's wrist and, before Priya could object, stuck it into her sari blouse.

'Have you gone mad?' Priya cried. 'What are you doing?'

Barbie held firm. Priya squirmed, and as she realized what it was she was touching she squirmed harder. 'Ai hai!' she yelped.

'Are you mad?' she gasped, genuinely worried.

Barbie smiled and let go of Priya's hand. 'Lovely,' she said. 'Good men don't grow on trees. They don't fall from the sky. And let's be franks, rarely do they enter Rassbery.'

'And this,' she touched her breast, 'this will fade. It will be okay, I know. But oh, you should have seen Raj's expression when I showed him. I could have eaten it! I would have paid for it!' Barbie's face was full with pleasure. 'It was worth it, Priya, I swear to you. It was worth it.'

Priya stared at Barbie. She had no words. Her bravado. Her chilli powder, her torch. How ridiculous she was! Priya wished her pitiful little weapons would disappear and that she could disappear with them.

What good was a torch on the body of a woman who would mutilate herself so grossly for Raj's affections? If Priya fought Barbie now, not only would she lose—'Who am I fooling?' she thought, 'I *am* a sickly twig!'—wasn't it likely Barbie would take a knife to another part of her body? What next? Would she cut off her entire breast? Scoop out her vagina to assure Raj she would never, could never, cheat on him?

Picking up her bag, Priya walked past Barbie and into the make-up room where the other girls had been following the fight, each with her own inverted tumbler against the wall.

'I'm not a beggar for love!' exclaimed Priya, throwing her bag down. 'She can have him.'

She stared at the girls with a challenge on her face. They stared back with pity.

∽

When I dropped by at Leela's two evenings later, she and Priya were still talking about Barbie. Their voices held a grudging respect. Like Barbie, and like every bar dancer they knew, they too were cutters. Leela chipped away at the skin under her Timex. Priya burnt herself. They would use anything—cigarettes, lighters, knives, pens, beer caps, the flotsam in their handbags, the jetsam in their make-up boxes.

But Barbie had taken something not even worth commenting on for those in the line and turned it into a moment that would enter Rassbery lore. She was so determined to get that *mangalsutra* around her neck!

The friends wished they were as far-thinking. As innovative. As brave.

Leela explained her cutting to me. Every time she felt thwarted—when Shetty wouldn't take her calls, and she knew it was because he was with his wife—she would drink. As she drank, the plunging sensation that had started in her stomach, tumbling and racing through her body, would begin to slowly dissipate. I had seen what would happen next. Leela would eat in grasping handfuls, she would crank-call ex-lovers, phone friends to insist they come over, badger those of us who were already there for approbation.

And then, when the euphoria died, she cut herself.

She cut deep, she liked bleeding hard. She would mock, 'Knives are good for slicing *kuchumber*, *kanda*. But also good for slicing wrists.'

Leela cut herself over Shetty because Shetty was married and would never leave his wife. Priya cut herself over Raj for, although he was single, he took her love for granted, regularly stealing money from her secret spot, under her parrot Chinki-*tota*'s food bowl. Every time he did so Priya cut herself in frustration.

These were the men they hoped would marry them.

'Do you know any bar dancers who are married?' Leela asked. She was hoping to explain, but she was also asking with hope. 'Properly married, the way you and your boyfriend will one day marry.'

No, I admitted. I knew women like Leela, who were in relationships with married men. Or others who had a live-in boyfriend they claimed they hadn't got around to marrying.

'Exactly,' sighed Leela. 'Men sleep with us. They give us money. They even take us to hotils. But the moment we talk of a proper marriage, your kind of marriage, they run away.'

'And it's not because we're used goods,' said Priya firmly. 'Is there a single girl in this day and age who can remain a virgin until she marries? It's because of our reputation. Men hear of it and want us only for sex and for money.'

Bar dancers did 'marry' though, as Priya and Raj had. Marriage to a bar dancer meant that she and her lover lived together in what they agreed was harmony. The bar dancer would refer to her lover as her husband. He would introduce her to his friends as their *bhabi*. Bhabi would fast on Karva Chauth; she wouldn't eat until she had spied the moon through her dupatta.

But a husband such as this was often no more loyal than a casual lover. At any time he would discard his 'wife' for the same reasons he had claimed to want her. For her beauty and her availability.

Then there was the sort of man known in the code language of the dance bar, in English, as a 'professional lover'. He pretended to fall in love with a bar dancer and after she reciprocated, beat her, cheated on her, stole her money and eventually ran away with whatever he could carry. He was such an experienced scamster, try as they might few bar dancers could elude a professional lover.

But even when a man wanted to legally marry a bar dancer and in return asked only that she give up the line, even then,

Leela was quick to inform me, the marriage wouldn't work. 'Such a man, what can he offer me?' she said, glumly. 'Okay, he's decent, he has a good heart. But for sure he's a simple-type who earns five thousand rupees a month, an amount he expects will buy me happiness. But how can it? Even if I tried to I couldn't stop myself from wanting things, more things, bootiful things. Eventually I will return to the bar. And the moment I do so, the man I married will leave me.'

And yet, knowing all of this, and not wanting to be deceived or abandoned, even then, neither Leela nor Priya would stay single.

A man would protect them from other men. 'Kustomers follow single girls home,' said Leela. 'And if she doesn't let them in they threaten to tell the police, even her neighbours, what she is.'

A man would protect them from themselves. You could never, ever, said Priya, underestimate what a relief it was to have someone waiting for you when you returned from the dance bar.

'To be held,' she said, 'even in the arms of a thief, is worth something.'

Most importantly, love was the only legitimate way out of the dance bar.

Falling in love and legally marrying one's beloved would absolve Leela and Priya of the loss of their virginity and of their sexual affairs. Marriage equalled redemption and would introduce them into respectable society. If she stayed single, Leela said, she would always remain in the eyes of the world a barwali. Years after she retired, she would be an object of suspicious derision.

Leela and Priya wanted to be rescued through romantic love, even though they had chosen bar dancing for the independence it allowed them to enjoy; independence, in particular, from men. This was one of the great contradictions of the line and of bar dancers themselves.

And so love was the constant in every conversation, an

audience to every silence. Thoughts of love filled the emptiness of Priya's evenings with Leela when the sun began its descent into the salt flats and with its vivid colours faded Priya and Leela's ability to lie to one another. The idea of love was a comfort when Leela suspected Priya was thinking of where her life was headed, and she worried that hers was going the same place because unlike 'good girls' no 'decent' man would have her.

Above all, the cutting was an expression of the girls' fear of what would happen to them if they didn't marry. If they didn't marry, they would have to work. And if they couldn't find a job outside the line they would have to remain in it. But not as bar dancers—soon they would be considered old—as madams.

Dalali, pimping, was the natural next step because no one was better equipped to sell women, it was believed, than one who had been sold, or who had sold herself. And no one was exempt.

Not the *kaali-billis*—the dark-skinned girls pejoratively referred to as black cats. Not the Bengalis who were 'dirty' or the 'Telugus and Madrasis' who had 'paise *ka lalach*'—coveted money. Not even the optimists who tried to make do by embroidering kerchiefs their children would sell on the local trains, five in five different colours for ten rupees, or the ones who married with little or no discernment, believing that marriage alone was enough, even if it was to the sort of man of whom it could be said with frank acceptance of one's fate, 'sometimes he works and sometimes he does not,' and 'one day at work, ten days at home.' And if one was in a nudging-winking sort of mood: 'My mister didn't go to work today. He drank too much deshi at our wedding.'

'Oh, congratulations, when did you marry?'

'Ten years ago!'

∽

Bar dancers like Leela and Priya hoped for a different destiny. A hensum man from a 'good bijniss family' would enter the bar, stop in his tracks in love with her and proclaim: 'Your past is past!' He would stretch his arms to show his love—this wide, okay wider, all right baba, as wide as the shores of Chowpatty beach! He would marry her in a temple and take her with him to bahar gaon, someplace special like 'Yurope' or Lundun. There she would eat fully well and nine months later promptly bear the first of many sons she would name not after her father who was inevitably a *haramzada*, bastard, but after her husband, who so far was not. Or, entranced by her beauty, that two-minute twirl she'd mastered, a famous Bollywood director would insist she star in his next film. He would promise in his *angrezi* accent, his new Mercedes SUV *ki* kasam, that the title would bear her name: *Priya Ki Aayegi Baraat.*

I wondered what the friends were doing to ensure the happy ending they wanted and deserved. How did they plan to make love happen?

'But love is destiny!' exclaimed Priya, taken aback. 'How can you predict when you will fall in love?' She turned to Leela with a disdainful shrug. 'Timepass!'

She turned back to me. 'You should just sit tight and wait for it to happen. Keep your mind fit with other things. Go shopping. See a good "fillum". Soak your hair with Parachute and sit in the sun. Accha, do you know Leela's paanwala is a part-time with the D Company? Oh and he has a white "pomerian", Laloo P. Yadav! Laloo sits in his lap and eats *meetha* paan all day long, can you imagine it! If nothing, he will keep you entertained.'

I have a boyfriend, I said.

'Really!' Priya said. 'Is he hensum?'

Very, I said of the man I would marry.

She assessed me.

Was I the sort of girl who could rig herself a setting? Sure I was hi-fi. Smartish in my jeans and silver watch. Skinny. But was I even wearing the right sort of bra? The pointy-paddy type that should draw attention down there?

She leaned forward to investigate.

And was that Vaseline on my lips?

Vaseline!

Priya sat back, flummoxed. Stepping out of the house with Vaseline only, imagine it! Let me tell you something, men want better than real life.

She decided to settle the question. 'Are you carrying a foto of him?' she asked.

I shook my head.

'Not even on your phone?'

I shrugged.

That settled it for Priya. A bored expression washed over her face. She ran her little pink tongue over those magnificent pearls searching for cavities that couldn't possibly exist.

Turning to Leela, she changed the subject.

7

'I too love you, janu!'

To take her mind off Raj, Priya became exclusive with one of her customers—a forty-five-year-old wine shop proprietor who lived in Mira Road with his wife, son, motorbike and an Alsatian he called Tiger.

Since Priya was a 'booty above average', explained Leela to me, she could enjoy dozens of lunches and dinners and was entitled to significant presents before it would be considered appropriate for the customer to introduce the possibility of sex with her into their conversations.

Sure enough, Priya reported that her customer was a generous man. Early on he'd slipped her a plastic packet, inside which was a bundle of one hundred rupee notes tied with string. 'He had no hesitation,' recounted Priya. 'Ration, kapda, shopping; whatever I wanted he said I could have. I had only to ask.'

I asked Priya if she would introduce me. Although I'd met a couple of Leela's customers and seen others outside Night Lovers, she always brushed off my attempts to speak to them at length. This was bijniss, she said, best not to get involved. I thought Leela meant it was *her* business and I should stay out of that part of her life. But I soon wondered if her reluctance stemmed from the fact that she didn't wish to spend any more time with customers than was necessary, or lucrative.

Leela's disdain for her customers was clear to them. When I attempted small talk, these men, often middle-aged, and seemingly educated and employed, would answer politely enough. But as soon as Leela joined the conversation, they lost all confidence. One got so nervous he began to answer my questions in monosyllables of '*Ji*'. Yes.

As in, how long have you known Leela?

'Ji.'

How often do you come here?

'Ji.'

Although Leela exercised every nakhra she had acquired through experience and copied from films, she dropped all pretences once she was sure a customer had fallen for her. Then it was for him to pursue her, for him to keep her happy. And if he didn't, well then, someone else would. Someone would always be willing to pay for Leela's attention, Leela said. To give her money even if it was money only for a smile.

'They think I dance for them,' she would say. 'But really, they dance for me.'

Leela was immovable on the subject and so I thought I would try my luck with Priya.

To my great surprise, she acquiesced. 'Why not?' she shrugged. 'Come eat with us at Pure Wedge. But don't you bring your notebook-pencil. Kustomer comes from a good family.'

ॐ

The manager of Pure Vegetarian didn't recognize me. He had, after all, been in a drunken stupor when we first met. He nodded briefly as I walked past him towards Priya, who was seated, strategically, under the air conditioning.

Priya's customer reminded me of a kindly uncle—he was short, fat and worried-looking. He wore glasses with old-fashioned, round frames and from his neck hung a gold pendant in the shape of an 'Om'.

I could imagine what was going through his mind—did all booties come with as much baggage as Priya? She must talk incessantly about herself, I thought with a smile. About Leela, and, mercilessly, about Raj. She had taken that first gift of money as indication that the customer's wallet was bottomless and I imagined she inserted a demand for a gift or a shopping treat into every conversation. If the customer demurred, she would caress his face and murmur, 'Janu, you know at night I dream only of you.'

His resistance would melt quickly.

By now even I knew Priya's lines and I would sometimes wonder how any man could fall for them—they were so clearly filched from the Bollywood films she favoured. But these admittedly disloyal thoughts evaporated when I saw her. Then I understood what Rumi had warned of, when he spoke of the intoxicating power of beauty.

Priya's customer stood up; he brought his hands together in a polite namaste.

'My friend,' said Priya with a smirk.

'My kustomer,' she said to me, jabbing in his direction.

To thank Priya for doing me this favour I had worn make-up. And whatever little jewellery I possessed. This pleased Priya, who was a natural aesthete, and she took me by my hand and made me sit beside her. 'You're looking smart,' she said, kindly.

'Yes,' agreed the customer politely. 'Just like Abu Salem's girl.'

Abu Salem was one of the underworld's most dreaded gangsters. His girlfriend, Monica Bedi, had been a B-grade actress before she gave up her career to live with him. Later that year they would be extradited from Portugal and jailed.

'Like you know Abu Salem,' Priya sneered. 'Or Monica! What do you know of Monica Bedi? As if you know anyone!'

'Nothing,' agreed the customer hastily. 'No one. It's just you said Soniaji was looking smart-si, no? I agree!'

'And the best comparison you could come up with was Monica Bedi? Are you trying to make insult of my friend?'

'No! No! It's just that . . .' the customer sat back with a thump. He began to nod his head like a helpless pendulum, '*Chalega,* hahn,' he surrendered, lapsing into silence.

I'm not offended, I said. I'm sure Monica is lovely.

'Loverly-shoverly,' grumbled Priya. 'She was in fillums; do you at least know that? What a chance she had yaar! And she gave it up to run off with a don. A donkey has more shit than that whore has brains! And what for did she do it all? The next time she'll be in a fillum it will be a fillum on how she ended in lock-up!'

A waiter with a creased shirt-front sidled up to us. Plucking a pen from behind his ear, he began to tap it impatiently against the grubby little notepad in his hand.

Priya didn't bother with the menu. 'One jeera rice,' she commanded. 'One black dal. And palak paneer. Also raita. And naan, three piece hahn. And one sweet corn, hot-hot.' She looked from her customer to me. 'And you two, what will you two have?'

At least Priya and her customer had one thing in common. They loved food. Priya wasn't joking when she said her preferred fare was 'wedge, non-wedge, Chinese, Mughlai, Punjabi and fish'. When the food arrived, the customer served himself first, tucked his elbows firmly into the table, and dived in. Neither he nor Priya spoke for the next twenty minutes.

I'm interested in the lives of bar dancers, I finally said.

'Yes,' nodded the customer. 'Priyaji told to me.'

I don't get a chance to speak with many customers.

'Most are illiterate!'

That's why I wanted to meet you. Priya told me how articulate you are.

The customer goggled.

Priya shovelled rice into her mouth.

How did you meet? I asked.

'In Rassbery,' replied the customer.

'In Rassbery!' Priya's head shot up. 'Is that all you can say?'

'In Rassbery, last Saturday of two months ago, it was evening time around 9 p.m. You were wearing a pink lehenga-choli with a ribbon in your hair and kajal in your eyes and you did a solo to *Mere hathon mein nau nau chudiyan hain* for which I'd made a special request, and when I asked your name you said,

"Aishwarya," and when I said, "so bootiful you are," and gave you five hundred rupees, you smiled at me.'

'And then?' said Priya, pleased.

'Then I held out more money and when you took it from me I said, "Is your name Aishwarya because you look like Aishwarya Rai?" And you laughed and, oh, how happy that made me!'

'And then?'

'Then I stayed and stayed, and I stayed until your manager sahib came up to me and said, "Sirji, why not return tomorrow? If we stay open a minute longer the 'polis' will knock for hafta." So I left. But I returned the next day, 3 p.m. sharp. I said to myself, I own my own "vine" shop right here on Mira Road and I have leased two more in Thane district. I work like a Bihari! Am I not entitled to some relaxation? So, no shop. I wore a new shirt, I rubbed some of my son's hair cream on my head, I sprayed perfume under my arms and yes, Priya, I came to you.'

'And again manager "aksed" you to leave because you were the last one sitting,' crowed Priya.

'Yes,' admitted the customer. 'I watched you from 3 p.m. until 3 a.m. I watched you even after you stopped dancing and I watched as you walked out of the door. Tell me, did you like me?'

'Huh!' Priya tossed her head. 'Like I'm hungry for love!'

'Did you like me?'

'What makes you aks that? Did I let you touch my finger? Not even when you gave me money did I let you touch an inch of me.'

'So? So, Priya?'

There was something determined about the customer's expression.

Priya held his gaze for a couple of seconds and then, without blinking, showed her talent. Wiping her hand on a napkin, she reached across the table and began to caress the customer's face. 'Janu,' she cooed. 'Would I be sitting here if I didn't love you?

Would I be sitting here if I didn't want to spend the rest of my life eating from the same plate as you?'

'I don't know.'

'Janu, are you trying to tear my heart into small-small pieces?' The customer waggled his hand. 'I don't know!'

'*Chalo* fine!' Priya pushed her plate away. It was almost empty. 'Since you doubt my love I have no reason to sit here. Come Sonia, come let's go from here. Might as well throw myself into a well! Should I do that? No response! Okay, done! No, wait! See this knife? Watch me slit my throat with it! After all, what use do I have of a life in which I'm not loved?'

She grabbed the knife in one hand, and my hand in the other, and made a great rustling show of getting up. Reluctantly, I followed.

'No!'

'No what?'

'No, don't go,' pleaded the customer. 'Please don't go,' he cried.

'Please cheeze!'

'Please Priya, I was only joking.'

Priya pushed the knife towards me and began dusting herself off like she was dusting off the customer's 'joke'. Sitting down, she switched on a terrifying glare.

'And then?' she demanded.

The customer didn't hold back. 'And then I returned home to my wife and first I thought, "How can I put her through this?" I'll be franks with you Soniaji—Priyaji was not the first woman I fell in love with after I married. There was another woman, also a bar dancer, her name was Pinkyji, Pinky Tandonji, and we were so much in love I forgot myself— she would sleep with me in my bedroom and my wife and son would sleep on the sofa. I forgot myself I tell you, and for what? She was a dayan! How much she stole! From me, from my wife's purse!' He hissed, 'I caught her stealing from my son's toy box!'

Priya sighed. 'Some women are so *neech.*' Base.

'Yes,' nodded the customer. 'But I too was naïve. I should have taken her straight to the station but my wife said, "It doesn't matter, at least you've come to your senses, and now she's gone what for to file a complaint and make a show for the neighbours?"'

'Such a good wife you have.'

'She's one in a thousand.'

'She's a diamond *na*?'

'She's pure of heart.'

'I wish I was like her, janu . . .'

'Priya,' said the customer tenderly, reaching for her hand. 'She may be my diamond, my darling. But you, you are my diamond, my emerald, my ruby. You are my one billion biscuits of gold. You are . . . you are my . . . my Kohinoor!' He sniggered. 'Priya, you're the Kohinoor the British couldn't steal. Huh, they stole our freedom, Priya, but they couldn't steal you, my princess!'

He was pleased. Now here's why a booty like Priya was with a beast like him. Further proof needed? He didn't think so.

Priya smirked. 'Janu . . . Keep control in front of Soniaji.'

You were saying something about not wanting to hurt your wife? I said.

'I *don't* want to hurt my wife,' the customer said vigorously. 'But arre, neither do I want to be hurt! Listen, I grew up outside Jaipur, Rajasthan, in a small village. We had no dance bars, no vine shops, no Pure Wedge, no girls like Priya. We barely saw women! Why, I couldn't dream that I would, one day, live in Bombay city. Might as well have dreamt of going to US! My father owned a small laundry *ki dukaan*; my mother was a housewife in *ghoonghat*. Growing up we didn't have a radio, never mind TV. We played marbles, grazed animals, counted monkeys, sheep, camels, parakeets, squirrels. Once in a while I would think about what I would become. I could take over father's dukaan, but only if my older brothers weren't interested.

Or I could start my own bijniss. What sort of bijniss, you'll ask? Father's dukaan was in the nearest town and so too Balaji's Photo Studio and Raj's Cycle Store and Golu's Tikiya Bhandar. Following? Like every boy in my village my ambition too was to one day own a shop I could name for myself, it didn't matter what I sold. And I wanted to get married because to marry meant I had achieved something. I was a man who could look after a family. Then I turned eighteen and my parents arranged my marriage. That first night I asked my wife, "What will make you happy?" She replied, "I'm as happy as God wished me to be." But I said, "No, tell me, what will make you happy?" and she said, "What will make me happy is a piece of gold for every year you are happy with me." Then I said, "What else?" and she said, "That will make me happy as can be. What else could I ask for?" But I asked her again and finally she said to me, "If you were to have a shop and to name that shop after me the way my best friend's husband named Pinky STD-PCO after her, that would make me very happy indeed."'

'Understanding?'

Not quite, I admitted.

'I'm saying that because I grew up in a small village, my ambitions too were small. All I wanted was to own a shop and to name that shop after me. And because my wife grew up in that same small village she too had the same small ambitions. Then we came to Bombay. I joined the merchant navy, briefly. I started my own bijniss. So now I have not just one shop but many, and I have a house and land. Why? Because my children must have a better childhood than I did—of playing marbles and counting goats. But what does my wife want? Tell? First chance she gets she scoops them up and runs home! She forces them to live in my father's house which has no toilet, nothing, why when we married my father took a big tin of paint and painted the invitation on the outer wall of our room: "You are invited to bless my son and future daughter-in-law on so and so date at so and so time, wedge dinner will be served." That is the life my wife wants for herself and for our children.'

'What he means to say,' said Priya, now alert, 'is that he wants to be with his equal. Someone who is independent, who has ambitions. Someone with whom he can explore the world, not hide from it. Am I right, *sonu?*'

The customer nodded. 'I love my wife, Soniaji, understand that. Anything she wants she gets. Forget one piece of gold, she has so much jewellery even her mother, so greedy she is she would eat gold if she didn't have so bad gas, even she has said to me, "Enough, son-in-law, no more. If you put any more gold around my daughter's neck for sure she will tip over and fall down."'

Can I ask you something? I said.

The customer nodded. 'Ask, ask.'

'You're with Priya, right?

He nodded.

You love her?

'Of course!'

'I too love you janu!' Priya preened.

So you want to marry her?

There was a pause.

'If that is what she wants,' the customer said, slowly. 'If what she wants is to break up my family, force widowhood upon my wife, wish for my child to become half-*anaath*, after all what court will give custody to a man who has left his wife for a, don't mind, Priya, barwali, then yes, to be sure, which temple please?'

I looked at Priya. She didn't love her customer. I don't think she even liked him. But after all he had said, after all that gibberish about diamonds and rubies, all he had for her was this?

Priya didn't disappoint. 'Have you finished your stupid interview?' she yawned.

Yes, I nodded meekly.

'Can you leave us alone?'

Yes of course, I said.

Priya gave her customer a delicious smile. 'Something meetha, janu?'

8

'I'm going to skin your flesh and throw it to the dogs!'

When the girls grew weary of the limited possibilities of their life in Mira Road, they would want to get out, even if for a brief time, and every once in a while that meant heading to the red light district of Kamatipura. Apsara was never invited along and had she been she would have resisted: Leela's mother was enjoying her freedom by exerting herself as little as possible. She left Leela's bed only for BC—Bhagwan, Bathroom, Cooking and Customer. So Leela would dial in for Chinese 'wedge fry' and noodles and, arranging the tin foil cartons on her mother's lap, say to her sternly, 'This time, mummy, don't call if you get lonely. I'll talk to you when I come home, understand? And I'll come home when I'm ready.'

That Saturday was a special one; the girls had been invited to a birthday party. The evening's hosts, one of whom was a brothel madam called Gazala and the other, Leela's close friend Masti Muskaan, were known for their flamboyance and generosity, and the girls expected a blowout.

Masti was a hijra—a feminine soul in a masculine body, a member of an ancient and secretive community described as the 'third sex'. But she was different from any hijra Leela had known. She was petite and pale and favoured 'western' clothes like dresses, skirts and high heels. She was also a bar dancer and had adopted Leela when Leela first came to Bombay, by offering her a bed until she found accommodation, and counselling her in the ways of their line. Their friendship grew quickly and Leela said of Masti, 'she is my true mother.'

Priya couldn't stand Masti. Masti wasn't castrated. She had a fear of flying and so flying to Thailand, where castrations were safe and inexpensive, was out of the question. And since she knew better than to trust her body to a *dai*, a midwife, she was 'bottom down', a man. So yes, Masti was striking, Priya admitted, but she wore men's *kachhas* and her kachhas were stuffed with her you-know-what. This, Priya impressed upon me, was unforgivably 'chee!'

∾

To prepare for the evening, Leela and Priya went to their neighbourhood beauty salon, 'Welcome, Good Looks'. It was run by an elderly Chinese woman and her four young nieces, all of whom had been born in India and had lived here since.

Leela walked in with pleasant greetings for the women she knew. Priya slammed the door behind her and towering over one of the stylists demanded: 'Arms—half wax; pedicure, fruit facial.'

'You do the facial,' she told a stylist. 'And you,' she commanded another, 'wax.'

'But I already have a client,' the stylist whined, looking up from the eyebrows she was attending to. 'And "lanch",' she rhymed it with ranch, 'what about lanch?'

Priya seemed sympathetic. 'Oh,' she said, her mouth forming a perfect O. 'Till now no *lanch*?'

'No,' sighed the stylist, her shoulders drooping, the moist thread between her teeth drooping as well.

'That's because LUNCH TIME IS OVER,' growled Priya. 'Duffer!'

I wasn't surprised by Priya's rudeness and not because she'd been rude to me. She simply wasn't a people person. Her attitude, despite what she might have wanted me to believe, had nothing to do with her appearance. Priya, like the majority of bar dancers when they interacted with those outside the line, was always looking for a fight. The limited experiences of the line and the extreme nature of these experiences—adult, violent, sexual and highly stressful—created a lonely and lasting trauma that made bar dancers feel constantly vulnerable. It was hard enough for them to deal with people within the line—managers, boyfriends and customers who judged them continually—but from those outside, the judgement was amplified many times over. They felt they had to prove themselves, prove, essentially, that they weren't sex workers. They resented this, and their resentment made them prickly.

Even so, Priya was an extreme, and I don't remember her ever mentioning any friends other than Leela. The only people she invested time in were Leela, Raj, select customers and grudgingly, and only for Leela's sake, me.

Leela appeared embarrassed for her friend and felt as though it was her responsibility to restore Priya to a good light. The salon, she whispered behind her hand, afraid that Priya would overhear and take offence, put Priya in a foul mood. It was 'local', that's why. Everything smelt. The salon—of acetone, shampoo and cheap dye. The stylists' hands—of aloo-parathas; their breath, of gum. They wore 'home clothes', which hurt Priya's sense of style, and spoke almost exclusively about food, specifically, the food in their tiffin boxes.

I thought this was a bit rich coming from the most voracious eater I knew.

'If these chokris are real "chinki",' Priya would grumble, 'then I'm the daughter of Hanuman!'

But Priya really disliked the salon because it wasn't good enough for her. It was a 'Family Salon' with 'Full AC', which implied low rates and respite from the heat, and the salon's best clients were often housewives between chores and gawky teenagers skipping class. Apparently these people reeked too—the housewives of perspiration, the teenagers of public transportation—and Priya referred to them as 'ugly donkeys' and 'monkey-cunts', and she loathed their presence like her opinion on the matter would effect change.

But for all her nitpicking Priya never did find another place to get her nails painted that summery lavender shade she so fancied.

'She *wants* to go to hi-fi places,' said Leela. 'The sort they have in Bombay, with girls in uniforms who serve you cold drinks and wash your hair with nice-smelling foreign shampoo . . . But she's afraid.'

Of what? I asked.

'That they'll know what she is.'

Leela became sad. 'So terrible no?' she said. 'Priya is such a booty, but all it gets her, all it gets me, is trouble. Men see us, they see whores. Women look at us like we're husband thieves. As though we'd steal what was forced on them—mota mader-chods and their endless demands! And their children? Huh, nothing childlike about them, let me tell you. They run after us calling, "Ai barwali, *zara nachke dikha!*" Bar girl, show us your dance! Oh it's so difficult outside . . . When we go to MD Lokhandwala for burger-fry Priya does English *ghit-pit* so no one will guess.'

MD was McDonald's, Leela's favourite restaurant.

Tell me, I said. Where did Priya come from?

I had never asked. She discouraged intimacies.

'She's khandani, from a village near Agra,' replied Leela. 'Can't you tell?'

How could I?

'She's so bootiful!' exclaimed Leela. 'Like her grandmother. She was a great booty, Priya said. She was a singer, a famous singer. In those days women weren't allowed to travel, but Priya's grandmother was invited all over to sing. She even went to Delhi! Her mother didn't sing. Why's that? Because only one daughter, the bootiful one, has to enter the line. Priya's mother married, and when Priya and her sister Patang were born they entered the same lottery system. The bootiful one would sing, or dance;

the ugly one could get married. When they were small they studied under a guru who taught them vocal music and kathak, even poetry. Priya could read, did you know that? Now of course she knows nothing, but mind you, that's by choice only.'

What do you mean? I said disbelievingly.

'She won't read,' Leela replied.

She won't read? I repeated. How can that be? Even if Priya didn't buy newspapers, how could she help but read words in front of her? Street signs and the names of dance bars, the Breaking News headlines that interrupted all her favourite TV shows.

'Addresses?' said Leela, bemused. 'What for would she need an address? She goes to the same place every day and she knows the way by heart.'

So she refuses to read?

'Priya doesn't see words,' shrugged Leela. 'If you put a newspaper in front of her, you will give her a headache. And why would you want to do that?'

'Anyway,' she continued. 'Patang won the lottery. She grew up to be kaali-patli-*dubli-si*; no one would look at her. She was allowed to marry and now she has two children and imagine this, they go to an English-medium! But Priya had grown from a bootiful child into a bootiful woman. And you know what they say, "*Jab tak* ladki *ke gaal pe* booty *hai, tab tak* ghar *mein* roti *hai*." As long as a girl is bootiful there will be food at home. So she had to work for the family, as a dancer. Her parents would take her to the zamindar's house, she would dance in hotils, she even saw Agra! Then she grew older and it was time for her "*Nath Utarvai*", the removal of the nose ring, as they call it. Of course, every man from near and far wanted to buy her.'

Leela jabbed her pedicurist's hand with her toe. 'Enjoying?'

The young woman shook her head nervously.

'That's okay,' Leela said kindly. 'Listen, listen. Maybe you will learn something useful. After all, in this world of men if one woman doesn't help another, we will all suffer.'

'Hahn, Nath Utarvai,' she turned back to me. 'Then Priya was thirteen and of course her parents first went to the zamindar. "Seal pack, sir, seal pack, pukka kunwari, ekdum zabardast." A pure virgin, absolutely fantastic. That's how they talk! Of course, he was very interested, but they couldn't let him have her at any altu-faltu rate. To raise the sale price of her virginity they had to raise the competition. The word was spread and soon men from all over the village, from neighbouring towns even, even from Agra, came to place their bid. Eventually some local bijnissman, not the zamindar mind you, some *Chamar-chaprasi*-chi-chi type who made his fortune in import-export, he won. Chalo, he who has money is king. Caste is irrelevant in such circumstances is it not? That night Priya's mother, oh she's a *Bhootni* No. 1 let me tell you, she got Priya stoned, on bhang. And then the bijnissman sent his Amby to pick her up. Priya was almost asleep by then, but still her mother went along—to make sure she wouldn't resist and force them to return the deposit. Can you believe it? Her mother was in the room when some old man fucked her double-twice? Yes, twice! *Kuchh bhi kaho*, Apsara may be simple-type, but she never watched me fuck anyone.'

Priya was sold? I asked.

Leela nodded, 'For full sex.'

For how much?

'Have a guess?'

A lakh?

'Five lakhs!' beamed Leela with pride. '*Paanch peti* baby!'

What happened after that?

'What would happen?' Leela said. 'She started going with men full-time. Not dhanda, mind you. After all she came from a good family, famous for their music and dance; she had studied. If men wanted Priya they would first of all have to watch her, be entertained by her. Everything else came later. But hahn, *baki* story like mine, same-same. One day she thought: "Here I am, someone's daughter, someone's sister, and these people, my parents, my sister, how do they reward my love, my hard work? By sending me to men and then not sharing, but snatching away my money!" So one day she ran away. She was fifteen, sixteen, who knows? She came to Bombay and this is where we met. I had gone to Rassbery; the manager is a good friend of mine. And there she was, Booty Queen No. 1!' Leela smiled. 'I knew we would be best friends, I knew it! Priya behaves like Mumtaz Mahal, but let me tell you she is no better than a child. Too sweet!'

And then she met Raj, I said.

'Raj!' Leela sniffed. 'Yes, she met him, they got married, their baby died. You know all that. But time passes, time changes things. Maybe with time our luck will change for the better? Who can tell?'

Once the girls were satisfied with the stylists' work, they hopped into an auto-rickshaw to the train station, travelling first-class in the ladies' compartment from the suburbs into South Bombay. Often, they would travel ticketless, not because they couldn't afford it, but because neither thought she should stand in queue at the ticket counter with the other passengers, most of whom were apparently of 'no kalass' and proved it by spitting paan or phlegm whenever, wherever, they saw fit.

From Grant Road station in South Bombay, they took a taxi to neighbouring Kamatipura, Priya riding shotgun so she could control the rear-view mirror to focus entirely on her.

To ensure 'max-joy' they began to fortify themselves with marijuana they had bought in fifty-rupee paper twists from Priya's shared boyfriend, Raj.

Raj was 'shared' because he was still seeing Barbie. (That Priya went with another man, the customer she had introduced me to, was irrelevant. That was her right because it was her livelihood.) Raj acknowledged the state of Priya's wrists, but he was impressed with Barbie's 'Chop Suey' breast as he described it. No woman had loved him so much.

Raj was a sturdy, confident fellow with thick, wavy hair dyed to match his light brown eyes. He wore tight pants with flared bottoms and satin shirts in bright colours. He worked in the branch office of a well-known insurance company, but as a peon, he confided. He served tea, carried files, modulated the air conditioning and when the boss's wife visited, carried her handbag and Pomeranian in a bag, to and from the boss's silver Lexus. Raj was aware that in the world outside the dance bar he was no catch. 'In this line though,' he explained to me, 'while a woman's booty is considered her wealth, a man's booty is the simple fact of him being employed.'

It was possible that Raj was waiting to see if Priya would go further in her demonstrations of love. But Priya said she wouldn't. 'What kind of man isn't satisfied with one woman chopping up her breast for him?' she wondered. That she didn't know kept Priya intrigued—she thought it suggested hidden depths. She decided it was worth sharing Raj for the purpose of plumbing these depths.

ᦔ

Kamatipura was named for the Kamati tribe of artisans and labourers who migrated to Bombay from Andhra Pradesh in the late 1800s, seeking refuge from famine. While their men laboured with concrete, Kamati women made bidis that took the entire day to stuff and roll and for which they were paid ten annas— six less than a rupee—for a thousand. By the 1900s, the state's apathy towards Kamatipura was visible in the absence of public lighting and a police force. The area was overcrowded and its migrant families suffered poor sanitation. They were ravaged with diseases, particularly venereal. In 1917, Bombay's police commissioner, the Englishman Stephen Edwardes, described these families as being of a 'low state of evolution'. Kamatipura's marginalization encouraged all manner of illegal activities including gambling and the sale of intoxicants, and in time the area came to be known as Bombay's red light district.

Not much appears to have changed. Kamatipura remains a

warren of brothels teeming with sex workers and madams, pimps and children, with their dogs and cats and goats and with raucous parrots whose language is as vivid as their plumage. Side streets of sweatshops are crammed with squatting men working furiously on sewing machines and with women threading sequins through saris in the flickering light of kerosene lamps.

That evening, however, life appeared less strained. Perhaps because it was the weekend, perhaps because more people than usual were celebrating birthdays, weddings, participating in religious festivities. I passed several tents pegged between streets and inside each one was a lavish shrine filled with gods and goddesses garlanded with flowers and ropes of twinkling lights. Giant speakers belted out dance songs, and the sex workers who could had gathered their children in prayer. Others went on as before. They unfurled their hair, powdered their faces and outlined their reddened lips with black eye pencil so their mouths popped suggestively and were visible from afar. Leaning out of their brothel windows in sari blouses scooped low and petticoats that clung, they called repeatedly and with unflagging enthusiasm, 'Ai, hero! Want some company?'

The red light district was divided into numbered gullies and by unspoken agreement each belonged to a single community. Female sex workers had their territory. Hijras theirs. Men had their territory, too. Like a pack of dogs, each group knew better than to stray, for the punishment for forgetting could be severe. Even if all you were doing was trailing around a corner daydreaming—of falling in love, of having the right one waiting at home for you patiently, monogamously—but say you were doing this dreaming-sheaming looking what they called 'heroine-like', making yourself attractive to customers who were, by rights, not yours, and say the ones who worked the street spotted you, then it would be within their rights to teach you humility. And they would, and then your gums would run like water and you would never again stray.

Having parted ways with Leela and Priya in order to explore

Kamatipura, I now sought to rejoin them. As I entered gully no. 1, I heard Leela before I saw her.

'I'm going to skin your flesh,' she was screaming, 'and throw it to the dogs!'

Leela was standing outside Gazala's brothel and the person she was threatening was a constable gripping hard at his lathi. Surrounding him like bullies at the school water cooler were a dozen hijras dressed for the party in saris, bangles and breasts. 'I'll piss in your mouth!' one of them warned. 'Your children will be hijras!' hexed another. 'You'll die a hijra!' screamed Leela with delight. She gleefully pinched a hijra standing beside her.

Leela was always up for confrontation. She thought it synonymous with passion. If a fight occurred in her presence, it didn't matter who was involved, or over what, she would launch herself in with gusto.

Leela took the side of the hijras, but Priya would have none of it. With her back pressed against the brothel wall and her silken hair billowing about like an unpinned dupatta, she played with her rhinestone-encrusted clamshell phone with an expression of boredom. A joint dangled out of the corner of her mouth.

Spying me, she waved me over without a smile. 'You wanted to know us better, Sonia,' she said, sardonically. 'Come, come. Have your fun. Take foto,' she taunted.

What's happening? I asked.

I had no intention of clicking photographs. A camera in a red light area is like a gun in a classroom. Something unfortunate will happen. The stage was already set for more drama than I was comfortable with and I didn't want anyone to think I was alone.

What's happening? I repeated, rubbing shoulders with Priya.

Priya resigned herself to being intruded upon. Using his lathi as encouragement, she recounted in a bored voice, that ugly motherfucker—she pointed a talon at the policeman—had demanded hafta from Gazala's hijras. While elsewhere he might have made his request bashfully, amongst sex workers and hijras the expectation of politeness was a fantastic one. Angered by his belligerence and edgy after a long day of preparation and prayers in honour of Gazala's birthday, the hijras had refused.

It was an unusual response, Priya said thoughtfully. Paying hafta should have come as naturally to them as squatting on the latrine in Gazala's brothel. Even the hijras were surprised by their response, and hooting, they made a run for it. Then brazened by the confidence of their head start, one of them turned to taunt: 'Hey, cocksucker, hurry up!'

The constable embraced the challenge. He caught up with the hijras as I reached the brothel. I memorized him, to be safe. He was short, skinny, pockmarked and aggrieved. His uniform was crumpled. A pair of sunglasses was falling out of his pocket.

Appearance notwithstanding, the constable seemed to know that he was better than the hijras and that it was his right to demand hafta from them. Even as they railed—'Money? I'll show you money! Look under my sari!'—the constable went on the offensive. If anything happened to him, he knew, as did his friends, where the hijras lived.

He pointed to a pretty young thing called Maya. 'Want to spend the night in lock-up?' he demanded.

'To meet my future in-laws?' Maya said cheekily.

'Take out a hundred, I said!'

'Ohho, a bribe?'

'Bitch!'

'Cocksucker!'

'You whore!'

'Maybe so! But even a whore like me wouldn't fuck a cunt like you!'

The constable rammed his hand into Maya's broad flat nose; his anger split open her lip, it split open her blouse freeing fistfuls of paper napkins like doves from a cage. As they settled gently on the ground I read what they said—everyone saw that they said—'Gokul Lunch Home'.

Maya's hand went up to her mouth. To be humiliated in public was one thing. It was a hijra's life. And it was the police most of all who loved to taunt their kind with catcalls of 'original or duplicate?' and 'what have you stuffed your blouse with today?' But to be stripped of her womanhood in front of her peers who would cry with her now and then laugh hysterically behind her back—intoxicated with the relief that it was she and not them, this time at least. On such a day. At her doorstep.

The constable stepped back a pace, and then two—but there was no way he could retreat far enough. His face turned translucent with regret. Or was it fear?

He had overstepped, he knew—not because of what he had done, but because he had done it on his own, without the buffer of his friends, to one among a dozen hijras. Now they would get their revenge, because he was alone, because he stank of fear, and fear was a stench the hijras picked up on immediately because often they stank of it too.

They crowded in, their breath hot, their voices harsh. Wasn't it enough they paid this sister-fucker a daily bribe of fifty rupees? Did he need his cock sucked as well?

'O son of a Kanjar,' screeched an elderly hijra with watery eyes. 'If you have shit in your arse speak up, speak up now and apologize!'

Just when it appeared the mob would have its way, we were startled by a shriek.

Now what?

I knew it, I sighed. This was Kamatipura. I mentally scanned the contents of my handbag—a pen, a bottle of water, a sandwich, my wallet. No possible weapons.

Then a hijra cried, 'Dekho!' and pointed to a shower of green and white sparks illuminating the clouds over Kamatipura. Then came a terrifying wail and cascade after cascade of golden stars poured like heaven's tears. More fireworks thundered past and now we saw no stars, no sky, but colour, all colour, dazzling colours everywhere we looked.

Ratatatatat went the fireworks, quietly went the constable. We watched him lope down the street.

'Just as well,' shrugged Maya, turning her face to the sky. 'If we had given it to him, we would have ended up in lock-up. If not today then tomorrow.'

'One way or the other,' said Maya, transfixed, 'we suck his dick.'

Spying me, Leela companionably linked her arm in mine.

'See how they bully us?' she grinned, pulling me away. 'But how we made his *hawa* tight? Ha! And did you hear what I said? "I'll skin you like a stray dog, make a parcel of your brains and courier it to your mother." Ha! Cunt ran faster than a cheetah!'

Flicking the joint to the ground, Priya shook her head at Leela. 'Happy?' she asked.

Leela nodded vigorously. 'So happy!'

෴

I had never been to a brothel and had no idea what to expect. Gazala's was straight out of a film. Her brothel was a baggy, blousy monster with four storeys and two small windows that glared down like glaucomic blue eyes. The interior exceeded my first impression. Drafts spun like tops. The stairs were uneven. The banister trembled like a bad knee. We walked into cobwebs, past rooms scooped clean of furniture.

Batting about were the hijra sex workers and they too appeared as though in a film. Maya's lehenga-choli, she told me, was from Chor Bazaar, a flea market nearby. The pearls she wore around her neck were a gift from a customer. She had tucked a peacock feather behind her ear, and on her arms she had, just that morning, tattooed the name of her father dead of alcoholism, of her mother lost to HIV and of the sister who had run away from it all. Maya said these things to me in the same tone I would have used to describe where I had bought the clothes I was wearing. She didn't want me to commiserate. I asked her, she told me.

So instead I said, you look beautiful.

She beamed, 'And you, you are top-looking!'

Stopping briefly to wash her face and reapply her make-up, Maya led Leela, Priya and me to an attic-size room on the fourth floor. It was clear from her expression of pride as she twirled around that she, and all of Gazala's hijras, had given it their fondest, most earnest attention. In the light of a single grimy bulb I saw streamers and on a stool a luscious cake fat with cherries. Placed neatly on the floor in order of height were paper plates, packets of savouries, bottles of Pepsi cola and Kingfisher beer and an Eiffel Tower of plastic glasses.

There were a dozen of us to start with and as Priya got busy with a beer, Leela was pleased to make the introductions. 'This is my friend,' she said of me importantly, emphasizing 'my' and 'friend'. Then pointing to an acquaintance, she would say in all seriousness, 'And this randi is called . . .'

Someone switched on Gazala's twin deck and the sound of tapping feet immediately filled the air. Leela whooped her way to the middle of the room and with a gorgeous smile began to thrust her breasts in and out. She jumped up and down, she twirled around and she was so full of joy, the other guests yielded to her. Leela leaned back, her t-shirt rode up, from her dark-chocolate stomach dangled a silver heart pendant that said LOVE. She stuck her thumbs into her waistband, she whooped louder and louder, and now she could have been a teenager anywhere, pleased with herself and with the attention she was getting.

The hijras looked on admiringly, but they didn't care to be upstaged on their own turf. They waited long enough to seem polite and then, catching one another's eye, agreed to make a play for the floor. Three of them, including Maya, spread themselves out and without seeming to edged Leela off the centre of the room and up against a wall.

'Arre arre!' pouted Leela. But before she could start a fight, Priya walked over and reined her in. 'Competing with hij's?' she scolded. 'Behave yourself!'

Gazala strode in.

I had never seen anyone like her. She was over six feet tall and covered in gold jewellery. When we wished her a happy birthday, she curtsied like we were royalty and boomed her thanks in the voice of a middle-aged man. As she turned to greet new guests I saw that the back of her sari blouse was stapled with streamers that fluttered, tentacle-like, all the way down to her ankles. Any other party and I would have wondered whether the theme was fancy dress. In her brothel though, it must be said, Gazala fitted like wallpaper.

Leela whispered that Gazala wanted only gifts of cash on her birthday. Other than the daily fee she charged her hijras for rent and food—breakfast wasn't included and lunch was a boiled egg— they had also paid for the party. That explained the hijras I'd seen idling at the corner of the street. One of them had said to me, not unkindly, 'Pyari, the money for Gazala's gift didn't pop out of my arsehole!'

In these hours, however, no one begrudged Gazala her joy. Leela's 'mother' Masti, who had entered with Gazala, started singing Happy Birthday. She had a voice like a trombone. We joined in, jostling each other and clapping all the way to 'many boyfriends to you' and 'you were born in a zoo!' Bursting with pride, Gazala blew out all forty-eight candles. She plunged a knife into the cream cake and we exploded with whoops and cheers.

As we sat on the floor eating cake with bendy spoons and sharing bottles of beer, I felt like I was among old friends. Of course, even my oldest friends have never displayed the transfixing curiosity hijras are known for. When they are comfortable with a woman, they sit real close and stroke her hair. They peek into her blouse to inspect the foreignness inside. In any other circumstance I would have left. That night, the pinching and prodding by Maya and her friends made me feel on the in. In time, I came also to recognize this communal trait as a compliment. Hijras may call themselves the 'third sex' but they want nothing more than to be womanly. Their curiosity about the female form is an example of this naked urge and expressed most unabashedly with people they like, and wish to be like.

&

Apropos of nothing, Maya, who was sitting to the left of me, murmured, '*Hijron mein himmat hai.*' Hijras have courage.

I agreed. It was as much part of their identity as long hair and saris.

'I was born in Kamatipura,' she said, placing her arm companionably around me. 'Why should I lie? I was born next door, in gully no. 4. My mother fucked men. Perhaps they were low-quality men? Who knew? But we hardly ate. I had to look out for myself. Who knows if I smelt? Bad people always found me. My teacher raped me. Then I was raped again. When I was ten years old, old enough to make my own decisions, I decided that if this was going to keep happening to me then at least I should profit from it, I should eat from it. So I stood outside the theatre, that one'—she gestured towards the window—'and I waited for men. That's when the hijras came for me. They said, "*Tum admi ko gaand marte ho, hamare saath kyun nahin aate?*"' You fuck men. Why don't you join us?

I had become accustomed to such confidences. My friendship with Leela convinced her friends to warm to me and, with their familiarity, they also honoured me with trust. Since so many of their friends had suffered similarly it wasn't often that they found a listener. So they were delighted to be heard and never reticent about sharing deeply intimate, even self-incriminatory details. Although I was shaken by their stories, I tried never to be discouraging. Sometimes it felt that simply by listening I was helping out.

Maya took my hand in hers. 'I cut my chilli,' she said, gesturing below her waist with a slicing motion. 'I was sixteen. It cost me thirty thousand rupees and robbed me of forty days of my life. For forty days, a dai applied hot oil bandages on my wound.'

How much did it hurt? I grimaced, putting aside my plate of food.

'If you live, you live,' Maya shrugged. 'If you die, you die. It's all God's mercy. You have to be strong, you have to be brave. The dai waits for the cock to crow four times and then brings the knife down with a *kachak*! I fainted! Later she sprinkled oil over me; she painted my blood over my body. Then she pushed my bottom into a stone.'

What for?

'Menstruation. When the stone pierced my anus I became a woman.'

And what about your . . .? I pointed, as she had.

'Some people like to keep it,' Maya said. 'But not me, chee! I said put it in a museum for everyone to admire, or throw it away so no one can. And that's what they did. They threw it in the water, safe from the stray dogs.'

You're very brave, I said.

'Agreed. Why, that morning itself, I remember it so well, my testicles were tied with twine and when it was time the dai asked her assistants to step back and she raised her hand and as I looked up at her do you know what I saw? A kite, same colour as the sky, and would you believe it, as the dai brought down her knife the kite wagged its tail and said to me, "Goodbye." And then it said, "Good luck!" Can you believe it?'

Yes, I said truthfully. I'd heard stranger things.

'Of course,' Maya added, thoughtfully, 'just a minute earlier my mouth had been washed with opium. That might have had something to do with it.'

Guests continued to stream in, they brought presents and good wishes, they drank and danced, and Gazala's outfit received unanimous approval.

Maya whispered introductions into my ear.

'That one,' she whispered, pointing to a young man walking

in with two women who looked like sisters. 'He has the best-looking girls in the bijniss. How does he manage, tell?'

How?

'He feeds them only tea and Gold Flake!'

'And that one,' she pointed to the elderly hijra, 'oh, hers is the saddest story, the saddest story you will ever hear.'

Sadder than your story? I thought to myself with wonder.

'She used to be a man!' said Maya.

So were you, I said.

'She used to be a proper man, I tell you! Not like me at all. I always knew there was something off about my . . .' she pointed to her groin. 'It was like having a monkey hugging my waist!'

'Not that one,' she pointed again. 'She was a man, a real man, up and down and back to front. And he knew it and was proud of it and was in love with a girl who lived next door to him. He loved her so much—*uske pyar mein goonga ho gaya*. He became dumb in her love. Their parents had spoken; the date had been set. But one day he discovered his girl was having an affair and he grew angry, oh so angry, angry like a thunder-cloud about to burst; and he warned her with the palm of his hand to never again stray or he would prove to her, he said, that his anger could discipline her as passionately as his love had freed her. But the girl wouldn't listen and, instead, she complained to her lover and they hatched a plan to get rid of this one forever. So one night the girl mixed something in this one's drink and after he fell asleep she took a knife and . . . *kachak*!'

I shivered. She was castrated by her own lover?

'At first I too felt sorry for her.'

And then?

'No more. If I embrace the sorrows of other people, even if they are people I care for, people I love, how will I live, you tell? There are too many of us, too many like us! I would suffocate!'

So she joined the hijras? I said.

'Not because we're wonderful people!' snorted Maya. 'Her

family must have thought, "No chilli? Might as well be dead!" So they dropped her off at medical and disappeared. That's where Gazala found her. Gazala has contacts, you know—in medical, at the police station. She can sniff out a potential hijra like you wouldn't believe.'

'Gazala,' said Maya, glancing over at her madam, 'we are so proud of her.'

ॐ

Later that night, Gazala asked if anyone had a final request. There was a mad rush for the shoebox of audio cassettes. Once the party ended, whispered Maya, Gazala would retire her precious Sony twin deck and no music would be heard in the brothel until the following year, on her birthday. If you wanted music before that, Gazala would say, you might want to learn to sing.

One hijra brought out the soundtrack of *Bunty aur Babli*. Another yelled, '*Just chill.*' But before any more claims could be made, Masti slipped a cassette into the player. She silenced us with a finger to her lips and striding over to the door switched off the light. The hijras put down the cassettes and quickly retrieved their spots on the floor becoming immediately still, shadowy figures in the pale light of the moon.

Asha Bhosle began to sing *Dil cheez kya hai* from the soundtrack of the film *Umrao Jaan*, a favourite with bar dancers, for Rekha, as the courtesan, was their icon.

In the song, Rekha performs a sensuous mujra to potential customers. As they are drawn into the web of her beauty and nakhra, the brothel madam, chewing betel leaf and sucking on a hookah, watches with a smile of lazy triumph. In a voice at once tragic and soothing, Rekha asks, '*Dil cheez kya hai, aap meri jaan lijiye. Bas ek baar mera kaha, maan lijiye.*' She pleads, '*Is anjuman mein aap ko, is anjuman mein, is anjuman mein aap ko aana hai baar baar, aana hai baar baar . . .*' The heart counts for nothing, you can take my life. All you have to do is agree with me just this once. In this gathering you have to return time and again, time and again . . .

I looked around and nothing I had seen before prepared me for what I saw then: everyone in the room was crying. Even Gazala. Gazala, her head on the shoulder of the hijra beside her, was sobbing.

To my left, Maya was crying. Next to her, Leela.

I assumed they were moved by the song, by memories of the film perhaps, for its poignant storyline was one, I imagined, everyone in the brothel could relate to.

Umrao Jaan is the supposedly true tale of a young village girl called Ameeran, who is kidnapped from her family by a vengeful neighbour and sold into a brothel. Renamed Umrao, the girl is trained in music, dance and poetry and becomes a courtesan. Over the years, she is successful, earning riches for her madam. Although she works hard to please, she misses her family and longs to be loved. But she's thwarted at every turn—the man she loves marries another woman and her attempt to escape ends in tragedy. When Umrao finally finds her way back to her village, she is shunned by her family. She has no choice but to return to the brothel, where she knows she will die a courtesan, alone and unloved.

I later brought up the incident with Leela. She responded with characteristic openness. 'I wanted to cry,' she said.

But why? I asked. Why were you sad?

Leela shrugged. 'The song took me home. I thought of people I had left behind. I thought of people I might one day have to return to.'

As the song died down, a moan emerged from the floor below. Leela forgot her tears and leaned in protectively. 'Don't worry,' she whispered. 'That's Gazala's latest *katatu*. His dick was sliced off a few days ago. He's been lying in bed since. Lucky mother's cunt gets to eat fish and meat for forty days, I hear. Forty days! *Mast* life I tell you!'

Mast life.

I thought about this.

I thought of an operation so dangerous it caused many hijras to bleed to death. Since they were, for all intents and purposes, orphans, their bodies were discarded in water or in landfills. Some would live through the operation but never recover their strength.

I stood up and walked over to the window.

The street was bare except for a few stray dogs, a few stray hijras, and it was still until a man emerged from the darkness and strode with familiarity towards the brothel. He walked past the dogs, curled into sleep and restful dreams. He walked past a hijra staring down at her feet. He sidled up to another, perhaps she was the prettiest. He whispered to her. Did he ask, 'How much?' She would have answered, 'Fifty, as always.' Did he say, 'I know a place'? She would have replied, 'Me too,' and perhaps that is what she did say, for she pointed towards Gazala's. He may have insisted she go with him, or she may have wanted to, to get away from us, intruders who had so audaciously taken over her home, for she started walking away, ahead of the man, the loose end of her birthday party sari trailing behind. The man poked her 'this way' and as she turned to him and paused, the wind ruffled her hair and light fell on her face, it fell on her lips and on the shadows under her eyes, it illuminated her bird-like neck with so many chains wrapped around it.

9

'The luckiest girl in the world'

The solidity of Apsara's presence made Leela irritable. Apsara tried to make herself scarce, but wouldn't leave the flat. At most, she would drag the TV into the kitchen, settle down on a *chatai* and watch serials for hours, sometimes the entire day. With her eyes on the screen, she mumbled and hissed, complaining about the weather and the price of vegetables, insisting that the women on TV were too 'advance' and that girls who wore 'boy cuts' should finish the look with a turban and tie.

Apsara left the LG on even when she knew her shakes and snores would soon fill the kitchen with their sturdy rumblings. Then she dreamt steadily, and once when I asked what she dreamt of, Apsara said it was always the same, of the time when she had, as a child, got lost in her father's fields. 'All it was was potatoes,' she said to me. 'Not neem trees or mango trees or apple trees that could hide from me the way home . . . Just small, baby potatoes flat as the soil itself.'

'And yet,' sighed Apsara. 'Yet I managed to lose my way. How? Why?'

In Apsara's dream the potato fields would turn into a field of trees, and when she sought comfort from these trees, extending her arms around a fibrous trunk, the trunk felt soft and clammy and she realized it wasn't a trunk at all but someone's leg she was embracing. And when she looked up, arching her head as far back as she could, she saw that the pair of legs went up to a waist and the waist to a torso and the torso to a neck and the neck to a mysterious . . . 'and that's when I wake up, every time,' she sighed.

Apsara also woke up when Leela walked in, even though Leela returned past midnight, even though there wasn't much to say between them, and Leela always refused her offers of chai.

Apsara would ask, 'Head massage?'

She would plead, 'Let me press your feet beti.'

Leela enjoyed living alone and she was finicky. She washed her steel plate, bowl and water tumbler soon after she ate her meal, but wouldn't touch Apsara's because she was afraid, she said, of catching gonorrhoea, called '*peeli bimari*' because one of its symptoms was a yellow discharge. The STD was widespread in the community and was considered socially ostracizing.

I wasn't sure if Leela really believed she could catch gonorrhoea from her mother's dishes. Or if she merely wanted to vent. Other diseases she claimed Apsara was a carrier of were 'fattness' and 'simple-type'. She was also a squirrel, Leela said; always on the lookout for secrets she could hoard and use against Leela.

In any case, it appeared more and more that Apsara could do nothing right, and so there came a time when she began with slow certainty to lose the small store of self-confidence she had accrued from leaving her husband and to once again cower when she heard footsteps approach the door. Then her daughter didn't call her 'saand' to be funny, she said it to be cruel, to convey anger at her mother's choices, choices that had pushed Leela into the dance bar.

'Here is my buffalo hump of a mother,' Leela would curse, 'and still no explanation!'

When Shetty unexpectedly invited Leela for a weekend in Lonavla, Leela jumped at the opportunity.

Lonavla was a crowded hill station near Bombay where many of the city's wealthy built their second homes. But it was primarily known as a getaway for lovers seeking privacy.

Weekends such as these, it was unanimously agreed, were best enjoyed in one of Lonavla's countless resorts of 'rain dance-disco dance'. There were swimming pools and in the shallow end guests held tight to the side. Into the pools gushed artificial waterfalls, thundering and roaring over rocks and flowers. The guests, women in salwar kameezes and saris, men in shorts and briefs, disco-danced, drank and made out.

Leela yearned to visit Lonavla and would drool over Priya's romantic accounts of drives in the chilly rain, of sex in front of a heat blower. Of walking through the shallow end of a pool, her hand entwined with her customer's. (She was learning to swim, confided Priya, but it would take a few more weekends to get there.)

Shetty's invitation couldn't have come at a better time. Not only would it be a break from Apsara's unbearable simpleness, but the invitation, it seemed to Leela, was an expression of Shetty's desire to take their relationship to the next level.

∾

Shetty drove up to Leela's flat in his navy blue Tata Sumo, and it said a lot that he was willing to risk being seen with her outside the dance bar, in daylight and in his car, the monthly payments of which, Leela knew, were being made by his father-in-law.

Although he was bald and barely came up to the steering wheel, Shetty made up for his shortcomings by being cooler than a *chuski*. He bopped his head to the music from his radio and as he swayed so did the stuffed chimp hanging from his rear-view mirror. Shetty thought soft toys stylish and he saw nothing peculiar about a man his age driving a car with a dancing chimp and a back window full of candy-coloured playthings.

Shetty honked once, twice, and then fiercely, a third time. He whistled for Leela.

Leela stuck her head out of her kitchen window and called

down excitedly: 'Coming, baba, coming!' She rushed into her bedroom and then skidding, turned back, 'Don't leave without me!'

Leela and Priya hurriedly finished packing a small suitcase with weekend essentials. This was Leela's first new suitcase and she had bought it in 'Bombay' the previous morning. It was red, her favourite colour.

The best friends laid down things that made Leela feel beautiful: low-rise jeans that showed off her delicate waist, heels to add height to her petite frame, new padded bras and panties in pastel colours and a pair of sunglasses that covered half her face, rendering her mysterious and hi-fi. She took along a wooden Ganesh for luck, a new striped towel for hygiene and a bottle of Old Monk rum for pleasure.

'Depends on PS mood,' she said to me. 'Everything is up to him.'

Before rushing off, Leela shoved her new Kodak camera into my hand. 'Take my picture,' she said.

I peered through the viewfinder. Fresh-faced Leela wore young girls' clothes—jeans with strategic rips, a clingy white t-shirt, white slingbacks at least four inches high.

She pouted, stuck her tongue out.

'Hurry!' she squealed.

'Chalo!'

I didn't know the name of the hotel Leela would be staying at. Wait a minute; I didn't even have Shetty's number.

Where are you going? I asked, lowering the camera. How will we find you?

Leela glanced quickly at her mother.

'So "sveet" girl you are,' snorted Apsara.

'Chup,' Leela said. She came over and put her arm around me. 'Why do you worry so much? Doesn't it give you a headache?'

'Planning to run to Lonavla if something happens?' asked Priya, coldly.

'Don't take tension,' Leela said. 'I can take care of myself. Better than this one,' she inclined her head towards Apsara. 'Better than this booty queen,' she pointed at Priya. 'And much, much better than you. So stop feeling sad, okay? Stop now I said, otherwise I will start feeling sad and then I'll cry and delay and PS will get angry and curse me. Come on, why don't you do something useful? Take my picture.'

She went back near the door and flashed me a smile.

Cheese, I said, glumly.

'Cheez!' Leela grinned, looking ecstatic.

The drive to Lonavla took an hour and a half, and if beginnings were any indication of endings, then Leela was in for a disappointment.

Shetty spoke steadily into his Bluetooth earpiece; he dropped names, cracked jokes, laughed uproariously. Swatting away Leela's Old Monk, he jabbed his thumb towards a box of Kingfisher beers packed into the back seat. Every twenty minutes Leela would pluck open another beer, fling the cap out of the window and hand the bottle to Shetty. About as often, Shetty would fling a crumb of conversation at her—something like 'maderchod weather,' '*kya* gaandu traffic yaar!' and 'you're the radio in-charge, okay?'

Leela fulfilled her responsibilities diligently, turning down the volume when Shetty poked her knee, turning it up when he showed his appreciation for a song by rhythmically clicking his fingers, and jamming mute when they reached the toll booth and for the fun of it Shetty asked the young man behind the glass screen stamped 'Do Not Spit Here' what he would do if Shetty refused to pay. The young man was not amused even though Shetty called him *dost* and Shetty turned belligerent as Leela knew he would.

Shetty considered himself a wit, but he had lost friends over 'jokes' that included prank-calling their wives and pretending, in a falsetto, to be their husband's pregnant mistress. Now he asked the young man if he knew who he was, and when the young man replied 'no' and 'what's it to me?' Shetty barked that he'd take his mother from the back like the bitch she was. He threw some money on the counter and revved off so fast Leela wished she'd listened when Priya had described where the seat belt was.

To calm herself Leela texted her friends, hoping perhaps that if she suggested she was having a good time, it would start to happen. 'Saw camel with orange coat!' she wrote. 'Boys dancing in waterfall!' 'Fudge jelly sweets for you!'

∾

But from then on, the weekend went downhill. Shetty had booked them into a resort called River View ('A Treat of a Retreat'). It had a swimming pool and a waterfall and offered a buffet of delicacies like pulao and mutton curry, golgappas and fountains of fresh, flavoured lassi.

Leela would have been happy to be a tourist, her camera slung around her neck. She had no need, she said, to dance to the loud Bollywood music a DJ in a bandana and shades was spinning, to stand under the waterfall in her new swimsuit and black lace leggings, to mirror the couples entwined in the pool— their love, their lust, a tangible thing it was only natural to want for oneself.

She could be happy, in a quiet, regular way, just being with Shetty.

'If he'd only sat beside me . . .' Leela sighed. 'But he was happy with his blue films and beer.'

When Shetty called Leela out on her glum face, she said what she always said when she didn't want to admit she felt low.

'I'm expecting my MC,' she lied.

Shetty was disgusted.

'Now you're telling me,' he roared. 'What were you doing before you couldn't open your damn mouth? And what should I do now? Make lollipops of your blood and sell them on the road!'

'Why are you talking to me like this?' cried Leela.

Then she shut up.

Leela was feisty, but she knew Shetty had earned his reputation as a danger admi. He had cracked a bottle on a bar dancer's head because she refused to go with a Chhota Shakeel man. He had then phoned the Chhota Shakeel man to apologize and to ask which lodge he should have the bleeding, wailing girl sent to.

'It's okay, durrling, not to worry,' consoled Leela quickly. 'We can do it, no problem. You won't even be able to tell.'

Shetty closed his eyes. 'Fucking randi,' he murmured. 'You're all the same you fucking whores. Lies, lies, nothing but lies.'

'How so?' Leela pouted. 'Is it my fault?'

'How much money did I put on your cell last week?' Shetty veered off.

'A thousand,' admitted Leela in a small voice.

'Then how come two days later when I asked, "Why aren't you returning my calls?" why did you say "PS, balance *khatam*"? Why?' Shetty leaned forward and gripped Leela's hand. 'Leela, tell me why.'

Leela blushed. That was an old trick of hers and she hated to be called out on it. She had a single phone but three SIM cards. Shetty thought she had just the one and as her 'husband' had promised to take care of her bills. On the first of every month, he would hand over the amount she asked for. But it must have occurred to him that most months he gave her as much as ten thousand rupees. Either Leela was spending the money 'talking sexy' to her customers, or she was spending it on 'women's things'—'abortions and suchlike'.

Which was it?

Shetty said he didn't care who Leela fucked as long as he didn't hear about it and lose face. Respect was more important to a man than money or power.

It irked him though that despite all he did for her—he paid

for her rent and phone, he bought her lunches and clothes, he even let Leela sweet-talk him into bringing kebabs for Apsara and hadn't fled when she chewed his ear off about what a good wife Leela would make—even then, mind you, Leela took men when she felt like it.

When Shetty was in a good mood he could laugh off Leela's popularity, even feel some pride in it—everyone wanted what he had. He would remind himself that he had, after all, never hired a bar dancer he hadn't test driven—front and back.

But when he lost the battle to contain his fiery temper, as now, all he knew was that he was a catch. He was a well-settled family man who owned his own dance bar, made great money and would, any day now, get a designation in the Fight for Rights Bar Owners Association (FRBOA), an informal union of the city's dance bar owners.

He deserved better than a woman who would drop her knickers for a five hundred.

The many beers during the long, hot drive, the embarrassing argument with that young man, so young he reminded Shetty that he was now middle-aged and obviously so, followed by the news that Leela was expecting her period, was simply too much information for Shetty to process. Unable to articulate his frustration at the collapse of a break he had looked forward to all week, he wanted to lean over and slap Leela hard.

He didn't like beating women, Shetty said. That was no kalass, he was firm.

He had slapped his wife once and the memory of that moment made him a smaller man in his own eyes. But violence towards his bar dancers, even if it was only the implication of violence, was unavoidable. Otherwise they would think him soft and cheat him by meeting customers outside Night Lovers so they wouldn't come in and the girls wouldn't have to share their collection with Shetty.

Violence then wasn't about kalass, it was bijniss. And bijniss was the oil on which his life ran with the middle-class predictability and the comforting security he had, as a child, been taught to aspire to and which, as an adult he had attained with no small amount of perseverance.

And just at this moment there was something about Leela, his damn bijniss, that made Shetty want to cut her down to size.

He told me what happened next:

He wondered how old Leela was. She had been thirteen when they had met, thirteen when he pursued her, fourteen when she agreed to be with him. She had been fourteen when he started looking around, fifteen when he found another 'wife' in another dance bar, sixteen when Leela found out and confronted him. She had been sixteen when he swore to be faithful, sixteen when he broke his promise, sixteen when he started looking around again. He hadn't kept track since.

But she had been thirteen when she had first laughed at his jokes, thirteen when he had wanted her, thirteen when he swore he would never stop making her laugh.

At thirteen her teeth had been like a string of Hyderabadi pearls fit for the neck of a queen.

Shetty smiled in recollection.

Leela thought it was because he had forgiven her. 'Get into your nightie!' she said to herself. 'Distract him duffer, quick! Make him forget this MC bijniss!'

Leela returned Shetty's smile; Shetty's face closed.

Her teeth aren't what they used to be, he thought. Of course, the dance bar will do that to you. Some girls! Their teeth so rotten, it was a wonder they tasted food. And their brains were no less rotten, mind you. *Angootha chhaaps*! Oh, but Leela. Leelaji could not only write, she could read. Once he had stumbled upon her reading a novel in the make-up room. There were very few things that impressed Shetty. That was one of them. Leela was so smart, just being around her made him feel good about himself. Like an upper-class man, in a top-class joint.

Of the many bar dancers who had come and gone from Night

Lovers, Leela was the one he had worked to convince to stay on. When her attention had threatened to wander he raised her cut of the collection. He allowed her to choose the song she made an entrance to, and in the make-up room she had her own dressing table, her name painted on the side.

It was a matter of luck, Shetty knew, that Leela had been forced into this line, a line that gnawed into you like you were the marrow in a plate of *nalli-nehari*, and once you had been chewed through and through, spat you underfoot. And that someone like his Mrs had been born into a good family and so enjoyed every privilege of respectable lineage—a good husband, a good flat, a good vehicle, good children.

Because the truth was, even in Bombay, that great equalizer, you couldn't always fight birth. And you certainly couldn't do it without money and without connections.

In Bombay, a nobody could die with nothing.

And in that moment, perhaps in the regret of that moment, Shetty regained his feelings of affection and regard for the young woman before him. And he wished, truly, that Leela—oh, bright as a blade, as quick-witted as a street *chokra* and as marvellously clever as a Gemini circus magician—had had better luck.

But she hadn't.

And young as she was now, she would not be young forever.

Shetty was not a cruel man; but he was a man with an eye for beautiful things. There was Twinkle, who was new to Night Lovers and ma *ki* kasam, she was so sexy. Things had been stressful lately, and he hadn't had a chance to test drive her. But he was tired of hearing about her from other men: 'Oh that Twinkle such a booty! I fucked her yesterday.' And of hearing Twinkle talk to the other girls: 'Saala chutiya! He kept moaning aah! Aah! Aah! Like I was sucking the meat out of his cock. It drove me crazy.' Clearly, Twinkle was waiting for something better—him!—and he was planning to get started with a bang, maybe take her to Vaishnodevi. He would give her the spiel: 'My parents died in a car crash when I was a child and I have been mother and father to my siblings for the past twenty years. I go to Vaishnodevi every six months to ask Deviji for strength. Tell me, sister, would you like to join me in prayer?'

'Yes, that would impress her. Why were these girls so taken by God anyway? Was it because God had given them nothing? Yes. Because they had nothing, they had nothing to lose.'

Shetty couldn't help but think about the last time he had been to Vaishnodevi. He had gone with Leela.

'All was going well, until I saw my brother-in-law walking ahead of me on the bridge. I ducked and weaved, but that *chut chataoing* maderchod not only saw me, he came up to me and said, "Hello!" and "Who is this?" about Leela. Of course, I said, "Saala gaandu," fucking arsehole. I don't give that bastard any *bhav*. I paid for his wedding. Let me see that money, then we'll talk. I said, "Is she your mother? Then why do you care motherfucker?" He ran. But of course he told his sister. Setting *kharab kar di*! He didn't even wait to get to Bombay; he called her from Vaishnodevi itself. She called me. Straight off I said, "Woman, what woman? Arre that poor widow? The stumbling, bumbling widow who couldn't manage her belongings? Yes, yes I helped her. What's wrong with that? Should I have pushed past without a thought? In a place of worship? Tell me?" She hemmed and hawed and so I said, "Mummyji, you believe your good-for-nothing brother who has always been jealous of me or do you believe me? Tell me, tell me now!" What could she say? She started crying, "Of course, I believe you; of course, you're the only one I trust."'

Shetty grinned. He'd fucked that motherfucker good!

His good humour was restored. He felt his muscles start to relax. He held his hand out to Leela. 'Sorry baba,' he said, pulling her on to his lap. Leela fluffed up with pleasure. 'Let's break the bed,' whispered Shetty.

Leela didn't dwell on Shetty's quick change of heart.

'Maybe his *nasha* wore off?'

It didn't matter. He was a man in a hundred. And he made her feel like the luckiest girl in the world.

10

'If I fall, who will accept my outstretched hand?'

L eela returned from Lonavla optimistic about her relationship with Shetty. To her, their weekend away signalled the
start of a bright new phase. Surely it was only a matter of time
before he suggested she spend the rest of her life with him.

To make her feelings on the matter clear, Leela no longer
went with customers. On the dance floor she became less likely
to insinuate the possibility of friendship. If a customer asked
for her phone number, instead of stalling, she would reply, in a
raised voice and in the hope that Shetty might overhear, 'My
phone number is my husband's number. Would you like my
husband's number?'

Leela's popularity didn't wane. Her customers thought she
was playing them and desired her more than ever. She continued
to leave Night Lovers with meaty wedges of one hundred rupee
notes tucked into her lucky red bra.

But Leela could be a soft touch. One day she hinted she had
a stalker. He would call at all times and make 'dirty-dirty'
suggestions. Give me his number, I said. I'll teach him a lesson!
'Uff, no!' she giggled. 'It's not so simple. He was my kustomer.
Then he got married and I never heard from him again. Chalo,
these things happen, no problem. Some kustomers become good
boys after settling down. Then it turned out his wife couldn't
have a baby and so he called to me and said, "Why don't you
have it for us, everything paid?"

"'Arre, arre!" I replied. "What do you mean? You have fun

and shut your wife up with a baby?" But he said she was insistent and that I had to meet her,' Leela giggled pridefully, 'so she could see how pretty I am!'

I was taken aback. And if you don't? I asked.

'She's a cutter baba,' Leela said. 'Why do you think I take his calls? Tomorrow if she makes pulao of her wrists, that *bhadwa* will chase after me.'

So Leela continued her philanthropic assignations with her former customer, sympathy, not sex, until Priya, with less than kindness in her voice pointed out that the man was fucking her over. 'It *is* like sex,' she stressed. 'Worse! If he has Leela's undivided attention, and that too free *mein*, he can put *nazar* on her.'

And then?

Priya sighed. She'd once said to me, 'We are same-same you and I. But you can read and write so you think you're better. But really, you're not.'

Now she indulged me. 'If he puts nazar on her she can get tan, get peeli bimari. Become a kaali billi. She will lose her looks and who will have her then?'

Purshottam Shetty? I said rebelliously.

'Sure,' Priya replied, her voice like cream. 'Because you know so many bar dancers who have married their managers, who now live happily ever after in some 2BHK in Navi Mumbai. Next time, do please introduce me to one of them.'

True, Shetty wouldn't leave his wife, even Leela knew that. Theirs had been a match consolidated by astrology, destiny and money. As Leela told it, before Miss Lata had become Mrs Shetty, her family had to prove that they were of the right caste and wealth and that Lata was as willing to commit to Shetty as she had been to God. The Shettys had been assured a car, a fridge, trunks of new clothes and, it went without saying, Lata's virginity.

Leela knew Lata had given Shetty children, two sons no less, that they went to an English-medium, had cellphones, liked cola and played cricket on the main road outside the cooperative housing society in which they lived.

'A co-op, imagine it!'

She knew Shetty was fond of his Mrs and loved his sons because he was eagerly planning their summer vacation. They were going bahar gaon, to Singapore, and the itinerary, Leela said with envy, would include 'shopping, Chinese eating, and the zoo'.

Leela knew all of this because she would torment Shetty with questions about his family; 'poke him' to use his words. She would eavesdrop on his conversations with his wife and read his text messages as though it was her right as his mistress. Since she was denied legitimacy, believed Leela, Shetty couldn't possibly deny her this.

Having gathered her information, Leela had come to this conclusion: to leave Lata would make Shetty a pariah in the Shetty business community. To leave her for a barwali would be interpreted as a sign of perversity. His parents would threaten a double suicide in a public place—a publicly holy place.

Although Leela dreamt of marrying in a temple, in silk, in gold, her palms embroidered with mehendi, a brilliant line of vermilion parting her hair, the tragic irony was that she had never herself attended such a wedding and drew her references from films (*Chandni*, starring Sridevi, was a favourite). And so she didn't fool herself and desire too greatly this one, possibly impossible dream that had so far eluded her and women like her. Instead, she hoped for the next best thing. A 'love marriage' in which she would be Shetty's sole dance bar 'wife'—not like she was now, but formally, with a party, for hosting a party signified enthusiasm and commitment on Shetty's part. To celebrate, they would kill chickens and goats and any altu-faltu type who raised timepass objections. They would invite everyone in the line and take lots of photographs, which she would make many copies of, preserving one set in her *Hanuman Chalisa* and carrying the other, at all times, in her handbag.

Shetty would continue supporting her financially, obvious. Most importantly, she would retire from the line and visit Night Lovers only on special occasions—when a puja was to be conducted, for example. Then she would tuck a Rotomac behind her ear, so no one would mistake her for one of the girls, and wear shiny new sandals under her Kala Niketan chiffon, so it would appear as though she had stepped from her flat into Shetty's Sumo and from Shetty's Sumo into the dance bar, condescending for barely a moment to tread on dirt. She would complain to those left behind: what a bore life is now that PS insists she enjoy, that she put her feet up in front of the TV and let the bai do all the *jhadu-pocha*-cooking—what else was she paid for, and how could the wife of a Shetty be poking under beds with a broom?

She would familiarize herself with this kitty party bijniss and, yes, send Apsara packing. (To secure good karma, she would book her a berth on an AC two-tier train and fill her fatty hands with mithai and some jewellery—'one piece gold, five piece silver'.)

Shetty could still sleep with whomever he wanted. He was, after all, still a young man, as healthy as a Punjabi farm boy, Leela said with pride. Leela knew the new girl Twinkle currently held him in thrall and she didn't care. She had it from a good source that Twinkle was carrying a particularly dire *gupt rog* and she planned to mention it to Shetty. 'It's the kind you get up here,' she'd say casually, pointing to her mouth, '*and,*' wincing, 'down there!'

ॐ

Leela's campaign involved getting herself tested for peeli bimari and other STDs, including HIV. Good health, she believed, was like pure gold—an obvious status symbol. Impure blood, Leela had seen with her own eyes, manifested itself in festering sores in visible places and in violent rashes that colonized the body like an army of ants. Some barwalis, she said, had reached such a crisis point, they had to slap dead people's hair across their bald heads.

Leela didn't believe she had peeli bimari, but HIV . . . This is how it is, she explained to me. When Manohar pimped her out, it was *pehle ki* baat, arre who knew of HIV? Then she was raped, remember, when she first arrived in Bombay? Do you think even one of those cockroaches wore a chocolate? From there she went to Night Lovers and back then too few customers had culture. The things she heard! 'I'm allergic to latex!' 'I deserve full pleasure!' 'Am I paying or not?' Of course, to be franks, in the minds of some girls there was no question of a chocolate, because they were on the pill and needn't worry about growing a baby.

Although Leela had been fairly careful since, it would do no harm to get tested. But yes, why hadn't anyone told her HIV could be transmitted through unprotected oral sex?

Since the previous year Leela had learnt more about HIV from an NGO that parked its mobile clinic down the road from Night Lovers. The first few times one of the *didis*, as the women who worked there were known, approached Leela with the suggestion of a check-up, Leela batted her away: 'I'm not those types,' she said, loudly bustling off.

'I was "proudy" with her,' Leela admitted. 'As though it made a difference! Sister's name was Baby, and Baby knew what I was. She would roam outside Night Lovers and every week she would walk up to me all smiling-like and say, "What's the harm, come meet our doctor. If you don't have time for a check-up, at least take some chocolates. They are free! And paan flavoured! Please?"'

The word 'free' did the trick.

'I liked the idea,' Leela admitted. 'So I went in. The doctor was nosy-like. "How many kustomers do you take? Do you have a husband? Is he your regular or does he go with his other wives?" But he wasn't writing this info down for the police. Only to understand how many chocolates I needed.'

Leela got checked for gonorrhoea. She was clean. Then Baby suggested a blood test for HIV. Leela agreed and went ahead. But in the weeks that followed, she avoided Baby.

'Your results are ready,' Baby would say, hurrying alongside Leela as Leela scooted into Night Lovers. 'Keep them!' Leela would hiss. 'Throw them away!' she said, another time.

'She became my shadow,' Leela recalled, resentful. 'Arre, if I didn't want the results I didn't want the results! What went of her father's?'

Why didn't you want to know? I asked.

'Some things are best kept secret,' Leela said. 'Some knowledge isn't worth the price you pay for having it.'

Shortly after the Lonavla trip, Leela was forced to reconsider her decision. It happened after one of the dancers at Night Lovers, a teenager called Ameena, fell mysteriously ill. Ameena was famous for her ability to dance with a pyramid of three tumblers balanced on her head. 'You could switch on any song,' raved Shetty, 'classical, disco, *Jana gana mana*! She wouldn't break one tumbler. She couldn't if she tried! Three years that girl was with me and not one crash, imagine it! She was a jewel, an angel. That first time I saw her dance I said to myself, "Purshottam Shetty, ready to be *crorepati*?"'

About six months prior to the incident Ameena started skipping work. When she did show up she was skinny, skittish and always coughing into the crook of her arm. Leela wondered if Ameena had tuberculosis. If that was the case, she hoped Ameena would have the decency not to dance next to her.

While performing one night, Ameena became visibly disoriented. She fell on to a table. It was embarrassing; she looked a fool. Shetty didn't make trouble. It was a one-time slip and he personally apologized to the customer into whose lap Ameena had spilt a quarter and several chicken legs. The incident would have been forgotten after a few nights of make-up room taunts, had it not been for the fact that, citing exhaustion, Ameena stayed home the next evening. And the evening after that, and then for a week until Shetty, who had a soft spot for his jewels, phoned her personally.

'Her husband picked up, of course,' Shetty said to me. '"Where's Ameena?" I asked. "Unwell," snorted that scoundrel. "But don't you worry Shetty sahib, I'll send her to you soon. This is just *natak*, you know. Sometimes my wife likes to do drama." This is how these men talk! And what does he do for a job, you may ask. Answer? Nothing! I bet you five hundred rupees had I visited their chawl that evening I would have found Ameena sweating from her tips to her toes, washing the floor, cooking food, feeding the baby while that useless nothing fellow would have been sprawled in front of their Sony TV yelling, "Ameena chai *la*! *Ek* peg *de*! Khana *khila*!" *Kameena* rascal! Idiot maderchod!'

One of the responsibilities Leela had taken upon herself as Shetty's 'wife'—unasked by Shetty—was to keep a tab on the other bar dancers. She would phone when they skipped a night of work. If they failed to answer she would 'take insult'. She would send off furious text messages, lashing out at their caste, character, the colour of their skin. When she needed a boost of confidence or wished to remind herself that she was better than her job, Leela would stand with a fierce face and folded arms by the back door from which the girls came in to work and rifle through their handbags for what she claimed was contraband.

'No drinks!' she would snipe, confiscating bottles of cola spiked with rum.

So when Ameena 'took off' once again, and four weeks later still hadn't returned Shetty or Leela's calls, Leela decided to do her duty.

၎

Ameena lived in Malvani, a cramped, congested suburb a local doctor once described to me as a 'dumping zone of people'. Malvani is overrun with chawls, prayer halls and dhabas you can smell from up the road. And its residents had demarcated its numerous enclaves as strictly as national borders, each with its own customs and characters. There were streets of working-class families and streets populated by hijras. In some streets lived bar dancers. In others immigrants operated brothels out of the tin-roof constructions they called home.

Malvani's most arresting visual, however, was not its colourful and varied communities of human beings. It was its population of goats. On entering the neighbourhood you might see just one and wonder what the big deal was, but before long you would know, because another goat would saunter into your path, and then another, and then you would, most likely, see a family—babies and parents dozing in the sun amidst a confetti of fresh green leaves, and then without warning it would appear as though you had stumbled into an enchanted city whose only residents were goats. There were dozens of them and they were of all heights and girths, and shades of chocolate, white and grey; they had silky, wispy hair and grand-daddy beards and collars they wore like necklaces as they promenaded unattended, knobbly kneed and elegant as can be past the very butchers at whose hands their lives would come to an end.

The chawl Ameena lived in was packed with people and goats and smelt of cleaning fluid and freshly cut grass.

'I couldn't see very well,' Leela recounted. 'Someone had strung clothes across Ameena's door and they blocked out the light. Pushing the clothes to a side I peered through and to the little girl sitting on the floor I said, "Baby, where's mummy?"'

'What mummy?' giggled Ameena.

'I jumped!' said Leela. 'That little girl, who I mistook for Ameena's child, was Ameena herself! How can I describe to you what she looked like? I saw death.'

Ameena confided she had HIV.

A few weeks previously, Baby had chased her down and because mild-tempered Ameena never could articulate a nega-tive, even to a stranger, she had agreed to an HIV test.

Now she was grumbling at the inconvenience her charity had caused her.

'It's bad enough that they admit us through a separate line, like we're of a different caste,' she said, of South Bombay's Jamshedji Jijibhoy (JJ) Hospital, where she had gone to receive treatment. 'Or that the ward for HIV patients is infested with mosquitoes. On one hand they say this is a disease of the blood and on the other, just imagine this, Leela, the place is full of mosquitoes sucking our blood and doing delivery service from one patient to the other! Accha, the last time I was there I saw policewomen in the ward, three of them. "What are they doing here?" I wondered. "Do they have HIV?" But no, they were with a prisoner and to make sure she wouldn't escape they had hand-cuffed her to the bed and were sitting on the floor beside her, holding on to her chains. They were police, what can you expect? They couldn't take the heat even for a few minutes! By the time I was ready to leave all three were snoring, loud as trains! I knew exactly what that woman was thinking—given half a chance she would have scrambled out of there, patli gali *se*!'

'Chalo,' Ameena smiled, 'at least I'm having new experiences!'

'So how do you think you got this HIV?' Leela asked.

'The doctor said galat *sambandh*.' Promiscuity.

'And your mister? What did he say?'

'Oh, isn't he my heera-moti?' beamed Ameena. 'Straight off he said, "Whatever my wife may do, she's never done galat kaam. I have full faith in her, don't say another word." Vicky is a *hamal*, coolie, you know, and he works so hard some nights I hear him talking to himself—"side *dena* side! Madam thoda right!" Just the other day he was saying we should move into a flat. Enough of this chawl bijniss, he said. How long are we going to live like the labouring poor? He may be a labourer, but wasn't I Malvani *ki* shaan, the most famous bar dancer in the line? "Why not?" I replied. "Our little princess should grow up better than we did. Do we want her playing with the daughters of pimps and the adopted sons of hijras? With dirty Banglas who teach their children-*log* to feed their goats at breakfast and to then eat them for dinner?" Of course not! Every parent wants what's best for their child, am I right or wrong? Well, maybe not my parents. And I guess yours neither! But we are different, isn't it so, Leela? Our children-*log* will have the sort of life we only dreamt of. What do you say? Don't you agree?'

Leela nodded.

'Well,' said Ameena, 'that's what we tell ourselves now. Accha, anyway, that's why my Vicky isn't home today. He's searching for a new place for us.'

Shortly after, Leela said goodbye to Ameena and, hugging her tightly, promised to return soon. As she walked out of Malvani, she happened to see Baby, who was on her way to Ameena's. They discussed their friend's health and then Leela, because of how things like these mattered to her, said, 'At least she has her mister.'

'Mister-twister!' mocked Baby. 'Her husband is keeping that woman!'

'What woman?' asked Leela, confused.

'Shehnaz, you know Shehnaz? Arre, Shehnaz from Rhythm Palace who lives with Ameena, cooks her food, washes her clothes. She moved in when Ameena was no longer able to, you know . . . She sleeps on the bed with Ameena's mister and Ameena and the baby sleep on the floor. Oh yes, that woman is sharp, sharper than the sharpest edge! Twice I've caught her with Ameena's mister, twice my dear, and you know what I mean when I say "caught". They weren't praying to Allah that is for sure!'

'Surprised?' Baby laughed at Leela's expression. 'Why, Leela? This is your line. These are your people. This is how it is, you know best.'

Baby proceeded to Ameena's house, leaving Leela alone with her thoughts.

'I had to sit down, right there on the side of the road,' she said to me. '"God," I asked, "what is this line you have condemned me to?" But Baby was right. Who was I to show surprise? I know how things work. Ameena couldn't have sex so her husband took it from her friend. And her friend gave it to him not because she loved him, but because she had to. He would pay her rent, protect her from goondas. My head began to spin. I began to think. I want to get tested. And I want to work on my relationship with PS. Because if something happens to me, who will I turn to? If I fall, who will accept my hand? And if my pain is so great the only language I can speak is the language of tears, who will lend me their ear? Tell me? Oh, this line!'

෧

The following week Ameena was back in hospital. Leela wanted to visit her and she asked me to come along. We were quickly lost. The reception was crowded and impossible to access. Even the stairs had been taken over by patients. Men, women and children slept on newspapers; they shook feverishly under shawls. The ones more able passed the time eating from tiffins, drinking tea, playing cards, reading aloud from newspapers and paperbacks. The hospital smelt of sweat and food and drink. It droned with conversation.

We finally found Ward No. 10 and spied Ameena lying on a bed next to a window. Although the ward was overfull, it was cooled by a lightly scented breeze.

Ameena was lying with her eyes closed.

Leela was right. She was so small, so rickety, she could have been mistaken for a child.

She must have been beautiful once. She had full lips and her thick, black plait coiled all the way down to the floor. But her skin was scaly and covered with a film of sweat and the pouches under her eyes were the colour and fullness of ripe plums.

Leela touched her shoulder. Ameena's eyes snapped open. 'Welcome, welcome,' she beamed, heaving herself up. 'Visiting hours are almost over and you are my first visitors today.' Ameena reached under her pillow and withdrew a tube of Odomos mosquito repellent cream. 'The mosquitoes will kill me if the HIV doesn't,' she whispered. She smeared her face and arms and handed the tube to Leela. 'Take some,' she said. Thanking her, Leela squeezed the tube into her palms and began rubbing the cream vigorously on her face, neck and cleavage.

I looked around for someone to talk to. A young doctor in a lab coat and jeans was standing a few feet away, leafing through some paperwork. Walking up to him, I introduced myself and asked about Ameena. He glanced over at her, 'She's come very late. Why didn't she come to me before?' I followed his gaze. Ameena and Leela were whispering to each other.

She's been here before, I said.

The doctor shrugged. 'She has HIV Wasting Syndrome,' he said, tucking the paperwork under his arm. 'She should have come earlier.'

HIV Wasting Syndrome is considered 'Clinical Stage 4', a late stage in the staging system designed by the World Health Organization. Other listed symptoms, as many as twenty, include Kaposi sarcoma and pneumonia, constant fever and diarrhoea. A patient with the syndrome could expect to lose more than 10 per cent of her body weight, which explained Ameena's startling thinness.

The doctor walked over to Ameena's bed. 'We need to get started on ART,' he told her.

ART, or standard antiretroviral therapy, is usually a combination of at least three antiretroviral drugs that inhibit the replication of HIV. They have to be taken every day for the rest of a patient's life.

Switching to Hindi, the doctor repeated himself to Ameena.

'It will help you,' he said. 'It's good medicine. You'll feel better as soon as you start taking it. Before we start though, we must run some tests—blood tests, X-rays, etc. It'll take a few days. Once the results are in, we can move on.'

'I haven't walked in weeks,' Ameena snapped. 'And you want me to wait "a few days"!'

'Counselling is mandatory,' the doctor said.

'Why? Why is it so? Is it because ART is something precious, something you cannot trust me with?'

'Is it a diamond?'

'Is it your wife's mangalsutra?'

The doctor patted Ameena's shoulder. 'We'll get started as soon as possible, don't you worry. I promise it won't take as long as it sounds.' He turned to another patient, lying on the floor near Ameena's bed.

I consoled Ameena. It's not a diamond, I said. But it's important, it's a big thing. It's a medicine you'll have to take for the rest of your life.

'Just a few more days,' Leela said, patting Ameena gently.

'It is a diamond!' Ameena whispered, staring up at the ceiling. 'Hear that, Leela? It's a diamond; that's why they won't give it to me.'

We left Ameena and shortly after that Ameena left the hospital.

She couldn't afford to stay, she told Leela when Leela called.

'PS is paying,' Leela said. 'Don't worry, it won't be on you.'

'Not on me?' snapped Ameena. 'Do you know how much the old witch next door charges to look after my child? Sixty rupees! Per day! And money doesn't fall from heaven, Leela.'

'Why can't your husband look after her?' Leela asked.

'How many things do you expect one man to do? He's with Shehnaz looking for a new place for us; I told you that before, do you never listen? He says now that I'm sick, I should stay somewhere better. No, you shut up! You and your finger-poking! When you have a man like my Vicky then you can start distributing *gyaan*. Until then, keep quiet!'

Perhaps Ameena was right; Vicky had been out searching for a flat, something away from their 'chawl bijniss'. But she would never know because he never came home and neither did

Shehnaz. When her next hospital visit was due, it was Baby who took Ameena, while a friend of Ameena's looked after her daughter as a favour.

Only a few days later things took a turn for the worse. Baby phoned Leela to tell her that Ameena was being transferred out of JJ hospital.

'Where to?' asked Leela.

'Where do you think?' replied Baby.

'Home?'

'She doesn't have a home, Leela,' Baby said. 'She's going to Trombay.'

In Trombay was a hospice for the destitute. Ameena would go there to die.

So what will happen to her child? I asked, after Leela recounted this conversation to me.

'What will happen?' Leela said. 'I'll tell you.'

'Someone has the child for now,' she said, as though to herself. 'But soon they will realize that a child is not a table, it is not a chair. It must be fed, it must be clothed, it needs toys. One day the child will go to school. What will happen? I'll tell you what will happen, because I have seen it with my own eyes. One day I happened to pass a *kachre ka* dabba and in it, not even deep inside it, I saw a dead baby. What had been a dead baby. "I'm losing my mind," I said to myself, "I need to get some sleep." And so I rushed off. It happened again. Another kachre *ka* dabba, another baby. "I'm drunk," I said to myself, running away as fast as I could. But I was not sleepy that first time, nor drunk the second. Because this is what I learnt, and I learnt it soon: a woman, if she has to, can bang her baby's head on the wall, *dhar*! She can bang it *dhar*! *Dhar*! *Dhar*! And once she has reduced it to *bharta,* she can walk to a street far from where she lives and throw it into the garbage. The stray dogs will eat her child. What they leave, the birds will eat. What they leave, is kachra. If a mother can do something like this, can you expect less of a stranger? We can pretend all we want, but ultimately the world sees us, why, our parents see us, as pieces of meat they can buy and sell, meat they can consume, meat they can throw away when it starts to stink.'

'Ameena will die alone. And mark my words, so will her baby.'

And that's why Leela decided to get tested again.

11

'I sell watermelons.
Watermelons and watches'

Leela considered other ways in which she could reinvent herself. Her fondness for *ayashi*, she concluded, would have to be addressed. A characteristic of the line, like dancing, drinking, cutting and customers, ayashi implied a hedonistic lifestyle in which one sought pleasure's tightest embrace. It was in acquiescing to ayashi's demands on one's body and finances that snatched from so many bar dancers their dream of leaving the line.

On a typical night off work, Leela and Priya would slip into hipsters and halters, spray perfume between their breasts and grab an auto-rickshaw to the hijra Masti Muskaan's flat fifteen minutes away. The shabby omelette-coloured building was Mira Road's party central.

Masti made no concessions as host; she didn't even wash her face. But at 9 p.m. each night she dimmed the lights in her flat, maxed the volume on the Windows Media Player of her ageing desktop computer and poured herself a whisky.

No invitations had been issued. Masti expected her friends, they always turned up. Bar owners and bar dancers, hijras and madams, pimps and small-time politicians chewing paan poured in.

Boys in acid-wash jeans came by to hang out with Masti's *chelas*, followers, their 'girlfriends'.

The guests were at home; they whipped out packs of cards, brewed tea, poured drinks and danced, sometimes with one another, at other times on their own, unto themselves.

At about 10 p.m., Masti's chelas Happy, Ramona and Gauri would be ready to leave for work. They would request Masti's blessings, blow kisses at everyone else and promising to return 'soon-soon' clatter down the stairs in their saris and sky-high heels. If Masti had been in an expansive mood, the driver of her white Ambassador—a gift from a former seth who had to mysteriously leave Bombay—would be waiting for them, holding open the door of the car.

Once they were let off on the highway, the hijras would instantly quieten. They would link pinkie fingers and their every instinct, like that of an animal in enemy territory, would be on alert.

Hijras, more so than female sex workers, were harassed constantly. Pedestrians mocked them, *'Teri kundi kitne ki hai?'* How much does your arsehole cost? Goondas would encircle a hijra, even in daylight, drag her to the undergrowth and take sex for free. Boys as young as ten approached hijra sex workers, less intimidated by them than by their female counterparts standing a few metres away. Hijras earned two hundred rupees for every five hundred rupees a female sex worker could demand for a 'shot', a sexual service.

Sometimes, there was no logic to the abuse. It existed because the hijra did.

Once Happy was hit on the forehead with a rock.

Why?

'Bindaas,' she shrugged, gloomily. 'I started bleeding, and when the man who had thrown the rock knew I couldn't get up, he crossed the road and peering down said to me, "What is wrong with you dirty people? Why can't you be normal?"'

The hijras finished up around midnight, and if things had gone well, if they had found customers and these customers hadn't turned violent, they would want to spread the buzz around. They would stop by the local liquor store. They would go to a dhaba, the kind that welcomed their business, and order a parcel of kebabs, rotis and biryani. You could never order enough for Masti's. You wanted to feel welcomed by Masti.

By the time the hijras returned home, Masti's guests would have spilled out into the corridor; a few might be so drunk they would be ringing other people's doorbells. Once a door was opened to them they would barge in and drag out sleep-bitten husbands and wives. 'Don't be shy,' they would say if one of the women insisted on changing out of her nightie into something more suitable. 'Consider us your family.'

Her neighbours didn't complain, because Masti was famous. And Masti was famous because she was loved and had been accepted by her parents.

૦৺

The Seths were a middle-class Hindu family. Masti's father worked in an office, her mother was a housewife; her brothers, as was the custom, would one day bring their wives to live with them in their parents' flat. As a child Masti, then Krishna, wore make-up. He stole his mother's bras. One Diwali, when he was about seven years old, he changed out of his new pants and shirt into one of his mother's saris. The Seths worried about their son, but they didn't discuss their feelings with him. They ignored their friends' prognostication that if they didn't take him to a doctor right away, he would be 'twisted' forever. When Krishna turned eighteen, he legally changed his name. He wore a wig, make-up and women's clothes. He was initiated into the hijra community and, as was the custom, acquired a guru to instruct and guide him through his new life.

The Seths didn't know any hijras. Like most of their friends they regarded them as pariahs and passing them by on the street treated them as such. But Krishna, now Masti, was so strong-willed they knew that neither pleas nor threats would change his mind. So they did, what they say, was the simplest thing. They went to the temple and asked God for advice. 'The decision came to me right away,' said Mr Seth. 'Krishna is my blood. Let him call himself whatever he wants. Let him dress as he pleases. Who can argue with young people these days? Yes, he's now a she. She's a hijra. But don't forget, hijras once occupied an important place in the Mughal courts. They were respected and feared. And these days, would anyone dare marry without the blessings of a hijra? My daughter has attended each and every big wedding in Mira Road, ask anyone! And not only as a hijra, mind you. She gets an invitation card!'

The Seths lost the approval of family members, some of whom they would never again see. And they lost friends. Mrs Seth said it was no big deal. If people didn't want to talk to her because Krishna was Masti, so be it. They weren't that interesting to begin with! And she didn't take her direction from those of the corporeal world, in any case. The holy books said that man recreated himself through his son. 'Masti is her father,' she said, simply.

The Seths weren't particularly well educated. Neither had a degree. And they would never describe themselves as liberal. And yet, when the need arose, they chose to be open-minded and progressive, to show compassion where others in a similar situation had offered only denunciation and despair.

'I have three children,' explained Mrs Seth. 'I had one choice. I could choose to lose a son. Or I could choose to gain a daughter. I am a mother. What could I do but what I did?'

Her parents' great love for her gave Masti great confidence. It also taught her empathy. When anyone in the building had a problem—with a neighbour or with the police—it was Masti who stepped in. And because she was beloved, on every major festival she was invited to inaugurate the neighbourhood pandal with the goddess in it. Her connections were wide-reaching, people whispered; they reached all the way to Bahuchara Mata, the Hindu goddess revered by hijras.

෬

As the night ripened, the intoxicants coaxed intimacies from strangers and made friends out of acquaintances. On one such evening, Priya confided that the customer she had introduced me to had died. I was stunned. He had appeared in his forties and although he had been overweight I would never have thought his life was at risk.

'We were shopping,' said Priya. 'And he fell flat! What did I know? I called his best friend. He told me not to worry, to stay where I was, that he would come soon-soon. It took him forty minutes. For forty minutes I stood by the side of the road with kustomer at my feet. Some people thought he was drunk, they turned their face and hurried past as though he smelt. When his friend finally arrived, he took us both to medical—like that would make a difference! Then he said to me, "Don't mind, Priyaji, but now you should leave. I need to call his wife and your presence will spoil his good name only."'

Did you hear from the friend again? I asked.

'Yes,' Priya nodded, 'he called me on his way back from the *shamshan* ghat.' Cremation ground.

'Kustomer had a heart attack,' she explained, for some reason running her finger across her throat.

You miss him, I sympathized.

She nodded soberly. 'He'd promised me a gold necklace for my birthday.'

As I paused to understand Priya, Masti's chela Ramona came up to me, her expression demanding my full attention. Ramona was petite, pillow-lipped and brassy-haired, and had recently returned from Thailand with a set of bowl-round breasts and, following her castration, something resembling a vagina, which I was told was decorative only and could not be used for sex. Ramona's breasts were a community treasure. She was one of only a handful of Bombay's hijras who no longer stuffed their bras with socks or napkins and so hijras from afar came to 'ooh' and 'aah' over her.

Ramona greeted me but ignored my hand because she was busy lifting up her kameez, under which she wore nothing.

'What do you think?' she chirped.

Lovely, I said, laughing with embarrassment.

'Touch them!' she encouraged, 'Go ahead, don't feel shy. Touch-touch, feel how firm they are!'

That's all right, I laughed again.

'Fine, then photograph me,' she insisted, refusing to wear her kameez until I had dug out my digital camera and photographed her topless. Every time I clicked, Ramona changed pose—she leaned forward, she pouted, she squeezed her breasts together.

'There's no point taking such fotos,' snapped Masti, walking past. 'You think a good magazine will print them?'

Relieved, I put down my camera.

Ramona jammed it back into my hand. 'Take, take!' She nudged her head towards Masti's retreating back. 'Poor thing. Her chapatti chest is giving her sleepless nights. Accha, after this, take foto of me in bikini. I use the bikini for my dance performances. I do bikini dance, pole dance, belly dance, group dance and cabaret. Want to see?'

At about this time, when it looked like things might get out of control, they often did. Someone would bring out paper twists of hash, one of the small-time politicians with 'hi-fi connections' might have a couple of grams of 'namak', cocaine. The whisky, rum and beer had long been flowing.

You could tell how long someone had been in the line, by their nasha. Gutka was always the first addiction. Then came beer, then quarters, and towards the end, brown sugar.

Leela was addicted to gutka, she enjoyed her evening quarter and her motto was 'if not now, then when I'm a mother of six?' So on nights such as these, she would always end up drunk or stoned, and on occasion her hand would find its way inside someone's 'husband's' pants and this would trigger a no-holds-barred fight involving bottles and kitchen implements and ma-*behen gaalis*, ending the party with the sort of finality that made even stragglers realize they would no longer be indulged.

When Leela spent the evening at Masti's she would lose the twenty-four hours that followed. It always took her that much time to recover. In a moment of repentance, she might grab Priya's hand, place it on her head and say to her, 'Swear you'll stop me after four drinks.' Priya would earnestly murmur, 'Saraswati *ki* kasam.' Saraswati, favoured for her fair-skinned beauty, was both girls' favourite goddess. But both of them knew well that unless someone imposed a similar limitation on Priya, Priya herself would get quickly drunk.

If Leela succumbed just once a month, then her ayashi would hardly be of concern. She drank no more at Masti's than she did at work, and it was only natural to her that like her nights at Night Lovers her nights at Masti's would pass in a staggered blur.

But she was drawn to Masti's every week, partly because Masti was her mother and she loved her, and partly because there wasn't much to do in Mira Road.

Leela's life was centred on making plenty of money and once she felt she'd earned enough for the week she grew restless. When she had time on her hands, she began to brood and more so than usual question where she would be in a few years. Sometimes, she said, it was like she was possessed by demons. The voices in her head would start to scream and then she had no choice, had she, but to drown these voices in a sea of alcohol?

She wasn't an alcoholic, insisted Leela. She would stop drinking the moment Shetty married her.

If Masti was at work or travelling, Leela would call Priya over for a drinking competition. They would push Apsara to a corner of the bed, lay out a bottle of rum and two glasses on a tray and blast a music channel on the TV. There was no purpose to this game other than nasha. The girls drank until they threw up or were nudged off the bed by Apsara who never let a moment of weakness go unpunished.

It was Masti who unwittingly helped Leela curtail her ayashi, during a weekend of what I imagined would involve prayer and meditation.

෴

Haji Malang, in the Bombay suburb of Kalyan, is the shrine of Haji Abdur Rehman Shah Malang, believed to be a twelfth-century mystic and dervish from Yemen. For ten days every year, pilgrims celebrate his Urs, or death anniversary, by laying a *chadar*, sacred cloth, at the dargah. Hindus and Muslims both gathered here, for the shrine was truly syncretic, with a Hindu and a Muslim priest each officiating at religious rituals. Like many shrines in recent times, most notably the Babri Masjid in Ayodhya in 1992, Haji Malang was at the centre of a menacing religious dispute. In 1986 the right-wing Shiv Sena party claimed Haji Malang as the site of a 700-year-old temple and demanded it be rebuilt. While the decline of the Shiv Sena's omnipotence in Maharashtra stalled this demand, the presence of *sainiks*, the party's foot soldiers, around the shrine asserted its continued interest. At the foot of the blue Malang Hills stood a Shiv Sena office, banners proclaiming the power of the Hindu state flapped between trees and men in saffron turbans swaggered, shouting their slogan, 'Jai Shri Ram!'

The shrine was of particular importance to Bombay's hijras—they felt an affinity towards the benevolent, all-embracing Haji. Hundreds made the annual pilgrimage.

To reach the shrine we had before us a steep climb of several hours. Steps had been carved into the hill, but many were a foot high, and as time swelled, so did my joints and they burned like an open wound. The route was as crowded as a Bombay street and to add to the confusion, everyone was walking, even bounding, at a different pace, forcing stops and detours. Mothers cradled babies, old men riddled with arthritis crawled like crabs and strapping teenagers, copycat CK briefs riding high on their bony hips, outstepped us all, keeping our spirits aloft with their playful jousts and off-colour jokes.

Leela ran ahead, she chatted with the teenagers; at every opportunity they stopped by one of the stalls set up along the path to enjoy a snack of peanuts and papads, lassi and sugarcane juice.

We were only halfway to our destination when the evening melted into a cloudless night. Now the route was lit by the light of mobile phones and in the hands of some experienced pilgrims, with lusty flares that sizzled blue fire.

When the end appeared in sight, it was without warning. Our group was reinvigorated. 'Haji Malang *jayenge to bahut maza ayega!*' Masti screamed, emptying out her lungs. When we go to Haji Malang we will have great fun!

We joined the chorus: 'Maza *ayega!* Bahut, bahut maza *ayega!*'

When we finally reached the pilgrim site, my senses exploded. I had never before seen so many jubilant people, collectively wired to their maximum energy. Thousands of men, women, children and hijras, dressed as though for a wedding, were singing and dancing and blowing on conches and banging on drums that hung from ropes around their neck, producing a sight and sounds so overwhelming all I could do was stare.

The narrow road was flanked by restaurants and shops that sold religious paraphernalia, snacks and sweetmeats, flowers and incense. A man stirred a giant jalebi into shape, his wife fried a puri as wide, as fluffy as a shawl. A young boy stood tall over buckets of red roses, his brother offered chadars of emerald-coloured silk and their parents invited Masti, Leela and me into their photo studio where we were captured in black and white, laughing with the joy of little children in front of the Eiffel Tower under a giant slice of paper moon.

The site was lined with lodges and the lodge Masti had booked us into comprised several rooms encircling a courtyard. Up a narrow staircase were three more rooms whose flimsiness was confirmed after an energetic hijra in pearls fell through the floor during sex with a little man in striped shorts.

Procuring sex, in fact, appeared as important a goal here as the attainment of spirituality. Or perhaps they amounted to the same thing, for as the night deepened, as the aroma of hash swirled in the air and spirits raised voices, confidence and desire, groups splintered into couples, couples who had hours previously been strangers, and they felt each other up in corners. Pushing aside the goats tethered there, they arched their backs against the walls of the communal toilets. All around the shrine, up and down the hill, the chill breeze gossiped of copulation.

Leela, Masti and I shared a room, and when we finally fell asleep it was from exhaustion.

I was woken up at around 4 a.m. by a rustling sound and stifled laughter. 'I'll bite your cheeks until they fall out,' Masti whispered hoarsely.

'I'll do kiss-kiss until you come-come,' a man growled in reply.

Leela woke up and when she figured out what was going on she started giggling. She giggled like she couldn't believe what she was hearing, when in fact she had warned me of just this. 'Never go on holiday alone with Masti,' she had said. 'She'll spend all day and all night having sex with every man who enters the hotil. Then she'll order room service. It's very bore!'

I need not, however, have worried about interrupting Masti. Although we were only two feet away, in a room the size of a closet, we were clearly no distraction.

Leela and I fell back asleep, and when we woke up we quietly gathered our things for a bath at the unisex *hamam* we had spied on our way in. We were treading over the sleeping bodies when Leela, in a moment of mischievousness or perhaps it was suspicion, drew back the sheet that covered the faces of Masti and her lover. Masti was shorn of make-up. She was no longer a curious beauty, but a man, just a man, and one with a prominent Adam's apple. But it was the sight of the boy, holding on to her like he was afraid she would leave without saying goodbye, that made Leela gasp.

Her face turned angry.

'Bitch,' she whispered.

'You bitch!' she raised her voice.

Masti slept on.

'Randi!' Leela hissed, running out of the room.

Nineteen-year-old Abid Khan, said Leela to me when she had calmed down, had been her kustomer—hers!—for over a year now. Oh, he was fascinating, she enthused, as we walked towards the hamam. He was writing a book!

On what? I asked, taken aback.

'Sex practices,' she replied. 'That Masti! She's a first-class randi more crooked than a jalebi!' Leela veered off. 'She doesn't deserve my friendship.'

But she's your mother, I said.

'I have a mother! You've met her! She's not much. But she's never stuck her dick into one of my kustomers!'

We started laughing and soon we left Abid Khan and Masti behind.

I had a feeling Leela didn't care about Abid Khan at all, just like she didn't care about her mother's 'simple type'. But I guessed that Abid Khan would become the excuse she needed to distance herself from Masti and the spirit of ayashi she so triumphantly embodied.

After a quick, cold bath we decided to explore the hillside. It proved to be a tough climb and soon I found myself cajoling Leela to change direction; to head downhill instead. Leela smiled at me like I should have known better.

'Just follow *na*,' she said. 'You'll see such things, things you'll never forget.'

So we continued on and first we passed a camp of pilgrims in varying stages of awakeness and sleep, dress and undress, and of these hundreds of people, while some bathed from buckets others cooked breakfast on makeshift stoves, while some tended children or animals, yet others were clustered in conversation, the rise and fall of their many dialects electrifying the air. Then I felt the clench, I inhaled the stench of death, for we had come upon the slaughterhouse set up for the pilgrims, and here stood stacks of carcasses, here flowed rivulets of blood. Then we reached the very top of the hill and I saw what Leela had meant. The view from the very edge took my breath away.

Trees small as a finger, rivers arched like eyebrows, hundreds, no thousands of pools of water, still, colourless and dreamy. And embracing this magical scene, and us, was the sky like I had never seen it before—a vast, wild roar as bold, as blue as the heart of the ocean.

∼

Later that morning, Masti and Abid Khan joined us in the courtyard for a breakfast of tea, paneer pakoras and jalebis. Masti introduced her new friend to us. Abid Khan was very tall and thin and wore tight black jeans. He was shirtless, but compensated for this with a collection of accessories including earrings, silver rings and a watch that hung limply off his right wrist. He had curly black hair that smelt of jasmine and he wore kohl in his eyes.

'Leelaji!' he said warmly. Leela responded with a grim smile.

Nothing about Masti's manner suggested that she knew she had upset Leela. On the contrary, dressed only in boxer shorts, her chest and face bare, Masti was radiant. There was a lightness to her I hadn't seen before and Abid Khan must have agreed, for he was as eager to snuggle up to her as he had been the previous night.

Abid Khan leaned forward, 'I'm a researcher. I'm researching sex practices.'

Is that a full-time job? I enquired.

'Job? What job?' muttered Leela, 'His job is *do* number *ka* kaam.' Smuggling.

Abid Khan ignored her. 'I sell watermelons,' he said, with a straight face.

Watermelons?

'And watches.'

You sell watermelons and watches? That's an interesting combination.

'He has his own truck,' explained Masti, animated. 'Say the police ask him to open his backside. What will they find?

Watermelons! Juicy-juicy! But if they throw aside the water-melons then what will they find? Watches! Foreign watches! From China and Korea, Taiwan and Sri Lanka—you name it, the world's finest watches Abid here sells!'

When he was not working the petty smuggling line, driving his truck across Bombay, selling watches he claimed were of solid gold and pure diamonds, Abid Khan pursued his research. He had conducted experiments in 'rose sex, nose sex, back sex, French sex, Italian sex, female and male sex, hijra sex and three-person sex.'

Very impressive, I said.

Masti sat back, pleased. So did Leela until she caught Masti's look of pride. Then her smile collapsed into sourness and she got up and walked away.

Do you visit dance bars? I asked, watching Leela's retreating back.

Abid Khan sat up. 'Barwalis are devil women I tell you,' he said vigorously. 'It's true what they say, "ladies' bar *jayega, barbad ho jayega.*"' If you visit a ladies' bar, you will be ruined.

How so?

'Arre, you go there for some fun, am I right? You have drinks, you become high, you become high you become "hawrany".'

Hawrany?

'Yes, wanting sex. Hawrany. You don't know hawrany?'

Uh. Yes?

'Yes, you know hawrany?'

'Arre, what hawrany-hawrany?' grumbled Masti. 'Leave her alone! Are you yourself hawrany the way you are looking-talking-making eyes at her?'

'No sveetie, nothing like that! I'm just explaining. See, you become high you become hawrany, am I right? You become hawrany you want sex. You want sex you need a girl, but these bar dancers, oh let me tell you, they are not of flesh and blood, they are entirely of nakhra! In a certain kind of bar, one of them will sit next to you and she will say, "Hello hensum, can

I use your cell?" or "Hey sveetie, how are you?" and naturals you get excited. But the moment you say, "Hello bootiful, want to come to a hotil with me?" she will start to make all sorts of sounds and faces like she's a movie star and you are asking for an autograph in the middle of her eating time. And her starting rate is so high an Ambani only can fuck her!'

How much would a girl like that ask for?

'Any amount that enters her head! Sometimes four thousand rupees, sometimes five, and that doesn't include the fee for the lodge and for all the food she will make you buy her—like she's a half-starved goat! And not only is she overpriced, she's much too sharp! Sharp as a drawer full of knives. Arre, what of that bar dancer who took full control of her "husband's" bar?'

What of her?

'She became boss! He became sweeper! Sweeper in her dance bar!'

He inched forward. 'Okay, can I be franks?'

Masti nodded on my behalf. 'Hahn hahn, bolo bolo. She's my sister, durrling. You can speak openly.'

'So the other day I get a call from this pimp, a real dirty guy. "Come see my new maal," he says. I said "fine". I picked up some whisky—why should I lie? His flat in Mira Road was filthy. And inside, sprawled naked on the bed, was a girl of no more than twelve or thirteen. She was marial, like she'd been starved. No gosht on her bones. I couldn't even look at her she looked so pathetic. I took out my wallet and threw two hundred rupees on her. Then I walked out. So what will this girl do? Sex work, then the dance bar when she's about fifteen-sixteen. Then Dubai to dance for gangsters and sheikhs. To fuck them. Get HIV from them. That's how it goes. At the end of her short career what is left of such a girl? Even if you wanted to love her, she wouldn't let you. Even if you offered her the world—car, clothes, cable TV— she wouldn't stay with you. She couldn't; she's no more human. She's a ghost.

'I tell you sometimes I feel sorry for these girls. But then one of them plays me for a fool and I realize *gayi bhains* paani *mein*, the buffalo has gone into the water. There's nothing I can do for her, she's a hopeless case.'

∽

When we returned from Haji Malang, Leela started her break-away. She would lie to Masti about why she could no longer come by. 'I'm having my MC,' she said two weeks running and so Masti suggested she get herself checked at the mobile clinic. 'Apsara is ill, she needs me.' At this, Masti screamed with laughter because plump, rosy-cheeked Apsara radiated good health, and even if she were wasting away Masti doubted Leela cared so much she would relinquish her partying for her mother. Finally Masti decided that Leela was snubbing her and she cut her off. Because she never did anything in half measures, she not only erased Leela's numbers from her phone, but, snatching her chelas' phones, from their phones as well. She would sniff when someone asked about Leela: 'Bitch is probably on all fours somewhere!'

Leela heard this and she cried bitterly. But she didn't want to end up like Ameena, alone even in death. She wanted to change— to make herself worthy of a good man and worthy therefore of marriage, even if all it was was a 'dance bar marriage'.

When Leela was ready to pick up the results of her HIV test she gave me a missed call. I phoned her right back. 'Come over,' she said. I happened to be in the middle of moving house. Can I come tomorrow? I asked.

'No! Don't come tomorrow!'

She immediately softened. 'I'll call when I'm at the doctor's. We'll find out together, okay?'

PART II
September 2005

'Now that you're unemployed, how do you feel?'

What happened afterwards was almost forgotten, because Leela lost her job. Rumours about a possible ban on Bombay's dance bars had begun to swirl in April 2005. Some bar dancers tried not to concern themselves with it, while others were in denial. Leela knew little, and what she knew she dismissed. In her version of the events that would change her life, 'a man in a turban appeared on TV and accused some fatso of demanding bribes. When the turban turned down his demand, fatso enforced the ban.'

'Turban' was Manjit Singh Sethi, the president of the FRBOA. 'Fatso' was R.R. Patil, the deputy chief minister.

'Of Bombay?' asked Leela.

Maharashtra, I replied.

'Turban was always on TV,' continued Leela. 'Shouting. Sardars shout a lot! He said Fatso asked him for a bribe in exchange for not shutting down the bars and Fatso said, "Nonsense! No such thing happened." But he went ahead anyway and announced that he was shutting down the bars because we were bad women—husband thieves! PS said, "Don't take tension, we Shettys are powerful." He said Turban was as chalu as any policeman and that Fatso was scared of him. "What of the bribe?" I asked. "We'll handle it," he replied. So I thought, "Okay, it's nothing to me." Apsara said, "Let's go back to Meerut." "Good idea!" I replied, "Go!" But she refused to leave without me. She's here to stay, I tell you. Curse my luck! Lots of bar girls went on TV, they went on rallies, they jibber-jabbered about how they would suffer if they lost their jobs. I thought, "They're hungry for attention—*bhookis*! Let them expose themselves. More kustomers for me!" And every time someone at Night Lovers spoke of the rumours I would bow my head and fold my hands and say, "You are a big person. You know everything. I'm only a simple bar dancer." Then came June-July and PS kept closing the bar without notice, and on the nights it stayed open the police turned up and PS paid them. One night, I remember so well, he got very angry with them, and with us, and told everyone, "Get out!" So after some *ghus-phus* the police left and we left too, even though I'd tried to talk to PS. But he'd gone inside his office and refused to open the door. And before I knew it, it was August and one day PS called to me. I told you this, remember?'

I nodded. He asked you not to come in for work.

'First I made a joke,' said Leela. '"Why? Did Twinkle ask you to fire me?" But PS didn't laugh. He said, "Go to Meerut. Or take a tour; go to Tirupati. And say a prayer for me too. In fact, you should go to Tirupati. Go with your mother and, if you like, take Priya with you. I'll give you the money." "But what happened?" I said. How hot he got with me. With me! He said, "Read the paper, Leela!" So that's how I knew that Fatso hadn't been joking. He had closed the dance bars. I turned on the TV and when I saw the news I thought, "Oh, I should have gone on a rally, I should have given interviews! Because at least I speak properly—not like some villager!" Then I thought, "No. Better I worked. Better I saved." And so the days passed, and then someone gave my number to some TV channel and a reporter-type phoned me and said, "Now that you're unemployed, how do you feel?" "Too good!" I replied and switched off my phone. And then, nothing. Turban got tired of shouting, I suppose?'

Sethi and some others decided to fight the law in court, I said.

'Court? What court?'

The High Court.

'High Court!'

'PS changed,' sighed Leela. 'Priya was over all the time. Apsara wouldn't move out. She said, "How can I abandon you in your time of trouble?" How could she not? My troubles would have halved!

'And then PS wouldn't take my calls. So one day I went to see him in Night Lovers. He didn't even look at me; he looked over my shoulder. "Leela?" he said, like he didn't know Leela was my name! And then he said, "My Mrs has palpitations." Just like that. So she had palpitations! What could I do? On top of that he said, "Learn to adjust." Learn to adjust! How much adjusting can one person do? Am I human or not? No one has adjusted more than me, let me tell you, and I'm not showing off, it's the truth!'

∽

The Bombay Police (Amendment) Act, 2005, was implemented in August that year. It banned dance performances in eating houses, permit rooms or beer bars—all synonyms for dance bars—that were rated three stars or less. In other words, while dancing was banned in bars like Night Lovers and Rassbery, it was permitted to continue in high-end luxury hotels. The bill had been introduced by R.R. Patil, at the time the deputy chief minister and home minister of Maharashtra, and it extended to the entire state. Patil had never before spoken up or against dance bars, but in April that year he initiated a campaign of vociferous denunciation, calling them 'dens of criminals' and 'pickup points' for 'prostitutes' that were 'likely to deprave the public morality'.

Patil's emphasis on morality led many, including the press, to conclude that he was using the idea of social cleansing the way some politicians used war: as a diversion from the downturn in every area of public life. More than half of Bombay's popula-tion, then nearly eighteen million, lived in slums. According to a report by the consulting firm McKinsey & Co., a third of this number had no access to clean drinking water. Two million had no toilet.

These figures were real to me: I lived near the beach, and every morning dozens of men and boys walked over from wherever they lived to defecate on the sand. Women came out at night.

There was nothing democratic about these figures. At this same time, Bombay was home to India's largest number of dollar millionaires. It was benefiting from an economic boom of 8 per cent and drawing comparisons with New York, Moscow and Shanghai.

The truth was that despite Bombay's sporadic experiments with intolerance it has traditionally enjoyed a cosmopolitan and animated nightlife. As early as the 1800s the French traveller Louis Rousselet noted with delight how 'the refreshment rooms in the city's taverns [were] thronged with Europeans and Malays, with Arabs and Chinese', and how 'far into the night the songs resounded'. City historian Sir Dinshaw Wacha wrote that the district contained 'a large number of low-class taverns', which he deemed as 'quite unfit for the reception of ladies' and 'populated by newly joined cadets'. In the 1900s, cabarets were en vogue and in the mid-1960s, the dancer Joyce Lee, alias Temiko the Tomato, was adored and is still spoken of among the older set, for in performing 'she left her breasts open to view'. It was during this time that Kamatipura flourished with brothels. Its sex workers were French and Polish, Russian and Austrian and they had come to the city by ship, and it was ships too that brought their customers—sailors who paid a few annas for their pleasure.

It was the liberalism and the politics of the 1960s that eased Prohibition and created what was known as the permit era. The policy change had been encouraged by Chief Minister V.P. Naik, a modern, forward-thinking, pipe-smoking Congressman who enjoyed the rifle range. The government revenue earned through liquor sales was doubly important because Maharashtra was dotted with sugarcane distilleries which provided molasses, the primary base for the manufacture of rum. Naik assuaged his more conservative colleagues by pointing out that the permit era would also curtail crime, ending the brewing, transport and sale of illicit liquor for illegal bars.

And yet, in 2005, despite the highly public resistance from the unions of bar owners and bar dancers, the liberal media and social activists, the bill that would ban dancing in bars received unanimous political support, across party lines. Less than a year later, however, it was repealed by the High Court on the grounds that it violated the dancers' right to equality and their freedom to practise an occupation or profession. The court condemned the government's discriminatory behaviour and directed the commissioner of police to investigate allegations that representatives of Patil had demanded a bribe from Sethi and the FRBOA. The state government appealed the judgment in the Supreme Court and the Court decided to stay the operation of dance bars until it delivered its verdict. When this book went to press, no decision had been made.

And so dance bars either shut down or fired their bar dancers and stayed open. Or they transferred their leases, resurfacing as banks, yoga centres or restaurants. Some dance bars chose to violate the ban and were able to do so because they paid the police five times more hafta than they had before. The estimated 75,000 bar dancers affected by the ban were largely uneducated and unskilled and had no work experience but the experience of the dance bar. The majority had to seek employment elsewhere.

The state government didn't consider it its duty to compensate these women. Having initially promised to provide them with alternative employment, Patil backtracked, claiming that more than 75 per cent were illegal migrants from Bangladesh. The claim was debunked by an independent probe. Patil then suggested the women find work as 'home guards' or under the

Employment Guarantee Scheme (EGS). If they didn't, he insinuated, it was because they lacked the will to do honest work for standardized pay. Home guards are volunteer assistants to the police and are paid minimum wage, which was then set at seventy-five rupees per workday. The EGS is manual labour, primarily construction, and also paid minimum wage.

The law targeted not just the women who danced but the licence holder of the space where the dance was being held. So although Shetty fired all of his bar dancers, including Leela, he was still open to threats and harassment from the police. Even women employed as waiters or as singers in the orchestra were arrested for 'participating in obscene activities'. So were their customers. Shetty thought it simplest to shut down. He didn't wish to appear to the police who were suddenly everywhere that he was above the law. What was more, he knew that once the attention of the public, and the press, died down, things would revert to normal. They always did.

Shetty hadn't thought twice about parting ways with Leela. The end, he insisted, had been some time coming. The trip to Lonavla had been a farewell gift. He thought she would have guessed, she was so smart.

Leela hadn't guessed, far from it, but she was quick to recover from this latest setback. Shetty had left her the way she would have left him in similar circumstances. With lies, without regret. She accepted his decision the way she did everything else destiny threw her way.

Jyotishji had said it would be kathin, hadn't he?

2

'Everyone drinks! Everyone beats!'

Priya's newest acquisition was called Tinkoo. He was her pimp. They had known each other a while; he was distantly related to the manager of Rassbery and was always hanging around. When Rassbery shut down, Tinkoo was adrift. He hoped to start a bijniss, preferably dalali. The girls he knew weren't interested. They weren't sure what they were going to do—wait out the Court's decision, return to their villages, or get into dhanda—but whatever it was, they had better options than untried, untested Tinkoo.

Priya thought so too, until she phoned her best customers. They taunted her: 'Pehle *nahin aayi thi, ab aana padega* free *mein.*' You wouldn't have us before, but now you must, for free. So she decided to work alone, on the street. She was successful and then one evening she was not. That was the evening 'something' happened. After that, she reconsidered her decision. Tinkoo had been calling and she had shrugged off his calls. He was a boy, her age. And he was 'soft', good-natured. That wasn't an undesirable quality in itself, but it wasn't much use in their line of work.

Then again, she had heard stories of real *dalals*. Not like Tinkoo at all.

That a woman who worked with a dalal would have to earn a set quota each evening, and if she fell short, she would be beaten. It didn't matter how much she earned, she always fell short; once her destiny was tied to that of a dalal, her enslavement was complete. All her dalal would do in exchange was arrange customers and book rooms for which she would pay.

He would throw three hundred rupees at her and send in such a storm of 'lund *khade log*', men with hard-ons, she would pass out after. And he went for quantity, which was why dalali flourished where alcohol and drugs were sold—once a man got high he wanted sex. When a woman serviced only men with addictions, it wasn't long before she was addicted herself, thus completing her dependence on her dalal.

Priya knew all of this. But she knew also that a woman, a young woman who looked like her and had never before worked the streets of Bombay, wasn't safe alone. What could Tinkoo do? If he acted smart she would give him two slaps!

So after giving it some thought Priya decided to return Tinkoo's calls. Tinkoo was so thrilled to hear her voice, so gushing, so grateful, Priya immediately questioned the wisdom of her decision. 'He's very young,' she sighed.

Leela had her doubts too. And not just because Tinkoo was a dalal, even if all he was was a wannabe dalal. He was a liar. He answered his phone sometimes with 'Pappu *boltoi*' in Marathi and at other times with 'Kaka spikking' in English. Was his name Tinkoo or not? She was also put off by his '*tapori*' style. His 'chadds' were always on display, for which she privately referred to him as 'Chaddi Bhai'. He dug name brands, same as Leela, but he had 'no culture'—the first time they met he was in 'Fendi', in 'Diesel'. He stumbled in 'Reebok' sneakers, a few sizes too large. Hi-fi people, Leela knew, didn't mix name brands. Further, each time they met Tinkoo pretended they hadn't before, to put her in her place, Leela assumed; to suggest her insignificance in his relationship with her 'jaan *se* pyari *jigri* dost'. Her best friend, more precious than life. It was his way of insinuating that she never came up in his conversations with Priya and so it was hard to remember she existed.

One afternoon Tinkoo went too far, asking Leela toothily, '*Tera* admi *kaun*?' Who's *your* pimp?

∾

I got to know Tinkoo over a game of *teen patti*.

Priya introduced us and she made clear that should I have any questions, I should keep them brief. She pointed out that the last time I had met one of her friends, he had died shortly after. 'I'm not saying it's your fault,' she conceded. 'But when you next visit Haji Malang, why not beg Haji to reveal your deficiency? Then one of the sadhu-bhais can recommend for you a lucky stone.'

Then I won't go around killing people?

'Yes,' she said, pleased. Finally, I was on the uptake! 'Then you'll be safe to talk to.'

Tinkoo laughed affectionately. 'Don't worry,' he said. 'She's not as *khadoos* as she looks!'

Tinkoo was a lanky teenager I assumed to be about Priya's age. He had wide brown eyes, a horsey face and a pierced eyebrow which was barely visible under his shiny 'flick', as he referred to it.

Not only was he unafraid of death, he confided, there was very little he was afraid of. Why would he worry? Know his past?

Priya rolled her eyes. 'He loves to talk,' she sneered.

၆

Tinkoo came from a line of famous pickpockets. His father had been a respected *chakri ka kalakar*, a pickpocket artist, who worked the trains on the 7 p.m. to 9 p.m. shift. He was so gifted he could switch between the roles of a machine and his assistant, the *thekbaaz*, on instinct. His favourite mission, as Tinkoo called it, was performed with his close friend Uncle Papoo. As an 'invalid' on crutches Tinkoo's father would fall as though pushed, and as he cried out in anguish apparently unable to gather his crutches, Uncle Papoo would pick the pockets of the crowd that had quickly gathered—not always, Tinkoo pointed out as though in justification—to help.

One night Tinkoo's father didn't come home. Tinkoo and his

mother wanted to believe that he had got held up at work, but that excuse soon rang hollow. Tinkoo's mother got tired of waiting and one day she left. She had found a man, she mentioned to Tinkoo on her way out. He would look after her, not to worry. Tinkoo was seven, maybe eight, possibly even nine.

Like the other unwanted children, and perhaps because he was his father's son, Tinkoo gravitated towards the nearest railway station—there was food to scavenge, people to rob. Yes, the station was full of thieves, and by thieves he meant boys like him but older, boys who thought it their right to steal from him because when they had been small, they had been stolen from too. So what? The station was a microcosm of the world outside. If you couldn't survive on a platform, what chance would you have in Bombay city?

Tinkoo hung around the big dadas, the thugs who ran the best scams in the station. They offered him protection and he ran their errands for spare change. In time, he made enough to move on. He was in touch with a distant relative who had made good and on his advice moved to Mira Road, attaching himself to Rassbery, where his relative worked as a manager. Tinkoo worked too, he worked the customers most drunk and disoriented. He would sell them marked-up cigarettes and in the process steal their phones, wallets and watches. If they were real drunk he would relieve them of their jacket, socks and shoes and hawk these items outside Mira Road railway station.

When dance bars were banned, Tinkoo decided to take advantage of the times and make serious money.

'Growing up on the platform two whisperings I always heard,' Tinkoo said. '"Ai, ladki *mangta hai*?" and "*Hame* ladki mangta *hai*." Do you want a girl? Yes, I want a girl. And so I knew that the best bijniss to get into was the bijniss of women. Because everyone, even hi-fi men, even men with girlfriends they love, want sex from the street. They think it zabardast. And they're willing to pay for it.'

Every evening around 7 p.m., Tinkoo and Priya took the train from Mira Road to the suburb of Andheri. At Andheri station, Tinkoo picked up his friend's auto-rickshaw on hire and drove with Priya to Juhu beach. It was poorly lit, densely crowded and thrived with sex workers. While Priya prepped herself, powdered her face and so on, Tinkoo solicited. 'I walk up and down as though I'm waiting for someone,' he explained. 'But what I'm really watching for is a man with a certain kind of look. A look of desperation, desperation for sex. When I see one, I jump. "Ladki?" I ask. If he asks how much, I say, "Depends on how much you want to enjoy." We agree on a price, nothing less than three hundred and fifty for one time, with condom, shirt and pants on, if you want alcohol bring your own but share with my Priya— she is, after all, going to give you full pleasure. We proceed to the auto-rickshaw. I drive slowly, but keep to the extreme left so that Priya isn't disturbed by the thought that people can see her. She's a very "sensitize" girl. She feels bad if people see her at work. And why shouldn't she? She has a good "repute".'

'Good repute,' snorted Apsara, 'says the dalal.'

'Dalal? I'm a secretary,' Tinkoo fretted. 'Like in Bollywood!'

'Do you know how Bollywood works?' he asked me. 'There are secretaries—it's a real job I tell you! Every big actor has a secretary. The secretary gets the actor films; a big secretary will get an actress like Aishwarya Rai a big film. In the same way, in Mira Road, I, as Priya's secretary, promise to get her kustomers. But not any kustomer, mind you. I guarantee the best of kustomers, the Karan Johar of kustomers!'

Priya snorted. 'Karan Johar!'

Leela laughed with her. 'Why Karan Johar? Why not Shah Rukh Khan?'

Tinkoo glowered. 'What's so funny about "secretary"?'

෴

The word 'secretary' made me think of Raj, who I hadn't heard about in a while. I asked Priya about him.

'Raj likes to eat and drink well,' Priya said, her attention on the card game. 'I could no longer afford to treat him.'

'You spoiled him,' scolded Apsara, throwing down a card. 'Every day mutton, every day fish. Did he even know the value of the food you were feeding him? Huh! So stupid boy must have thought the fish swam directly from the sea on to his plate.'

'After I lost my job he supported me for a few days,' Priya said. 'And then he said to me, even though he was living in my flat, "You think this is a dharamshala? Do what you want, I need five hundred rupees from you per day. Paise mangta *hai toh* mangta *hai*."' I need money means I need money.

'He was a perfectly good fellow before he met you,' said Apsara, her brow furrowed. 'He had a job! You girls spoil all the good men with your ways and your money. You fill them with greed. Now look at him! No better than a footpath *ka* goonda running after any randi who will have him and on whose money he can eat. Khana, *daru peena, masti karna*, that's his life! Thanks to you!'

'I couldn't come up with a hundred, let alone five. And so one day he said to me, "I'm getting bore of you," and I haven't seen him since.'

'Haven't seen him since!' Apsara glared. 'He started beating you because you stopped giving him money, why don't you say so? Admit he drank and beat you, where's the shame? Admit it!'

'Everyone drinks!' Priya snapped, refusing to meet Apsara's eye. 'Everyone beats!'

'But he beat you like you were a dog!'

Priya turned to me. 'I tried to make money so he would stay.'

How? I asked.

'I tried to do dalali for myself—but zero, it gave me zero income. So I asked the other girls for advice. My friend Poonam had a good spot in Santacruz, in front of the children's park, do you know the one with the giant plane? Opposite the police station? She felt safe she said, as long as she paid the police on time. She would share her place with me—no police, no pimp, no problem. I went with her.'

'Such a sad story,' said Apsara. 'Every time I think about it I want to cry.'

'Then cry!' Leela slapped a card down.

'What's the purpose?' Apsara clawed back. 'Has she not walked down that gully already?'

'You know best a woman can't live in peace!'

'She fed him!'

'But first he fed her!'

'Huh! Ten years ago he fed her for a few days. And didn't she feed him since, like he was a king—Mira Road *ka Shahenshah*?'

'She loved him mummy! How is this her fault?'

'I won't say!'

They were like junkies suffering withdrawal.

Tinkoo looked worriedly from mother to daughter and came quickly to a decision. 'I have a meeting,' he announced, flicking.

He shook hands with me, nodded at the others and hastily slipped out of the door.

So, what happened? I turned to Priya.

She shook her head, 'It doesn't matter.'

It does to me.

'It's no breaking news.'

I don't mind.

'What's to tell?' Priya shrugged. 'Poonam said she would accompany me until I got confident. But I told her, "What to worry? I'm not attending a surprise birthday party." And I was all right the first day and the second. Then on the third day around 8 p.m. a taxi pulled up and in the back seat was a man, young and well spoken—so don't blame me Aunty! He said to me, "*Jaane ka*?" Naturally I replied, "That's why I'm standing here." We decided on Guru Lodge in Khar. Poonam said, "I'll come with you!" But I was feeling confident-like, so I said, "Why bother?" I thought she wanted a cut because she had helped me out and because the man looked like he was from a good family. He was in a taxi. He seemed educated. You'll laugh now, but my first thought was: "How to get this shiny mister to fall in love with me?" Ha. Anyway, Poonam insisted and she got in. Barely fifty feet down the road, the man asked the driver to stop and four more men jumped into the taxi. The man stuck a knife into my side and warned me not to shout. The taxi driver pretended he was blind. Poonam said straight off, "I have a son. Rape me, ten times rape me, but don't snatch my life." As if they were after her life. Never mind Khar, they drove for two hours, all the way to a lodge in Aksa Beach. The entire night they drank and raped us. We didn't get a minute's rest. I managed to call the reception, but the person who answered said to me, "You came from the road, no? Why don't you take your problems back there?"'

'What had she done to deserve this?' Apsara said, scanning the cards in her hand. 'Nothing?' she asked, picking one.

Priya ignored her. 'Do you know what I call that night? Bhagwan *ki dua*. I know of a dhandewali who was picked up like this by ten men. Ten! Ten men cannot rent one room. They went to the closest jungle. They raped her. After they finished, they raped her with beer bottles. Then they left her to die.'

Apsara looked up. 'Don't talk of unholy things.'

'It's not unholy if it's true.'

'Girls are dying,' Apsara said to me, lowering her voice like she was sharing a confidence.

I nodded. In recent, unrelated incidents two bar dancers had died in a single week. Meena Ramu T. had been twenty-two when she hung herself. Bilkish Sahu had been twenty-four and pregnant with her second child. The press speculated that both deaths were connected to the women's recent unemployment due to the ban.

'Why are you scared of death?' Leela said to her mother, curiously.

'Talk of death like you're talking about lunch, why don't you?' Apsara hissed.

'You are scared of everything,' Leela concluded. '*Darpok*,' she whispered behind her cards.

'Anyway,' said Priya. 'That's when I decided I wouldn't work alone. Better to work with a boy, a Tinkoo-type boy, than to work as an alone girl in this city.'

I asked Priya if she would talk to someone about what had happened. I had a rape counsellor in mind, a doctor. She dismissed me. Apsara and Leela continued with their card game as though they hadn't heard.

∾

But even I knew better than to suggest a visit to the police. Priya and Leela had always feared them, but since she had begun working with Tinkoo, Priya paid the police hafta without them having to ask for it. She was now a sex worker and sex work was technically illegal. 'They told me to buy a notebook,' she said to me, 'and every time I submit hafta to make sure they sign in it, so they cannot force me to pay them more than once a week. They're fair-minded, they said. No exploitation.'

The payment was to avoid arrest and that was all Priya could buy, for no policeman would let pass an opportunity to ask in a voice loud enough for everyone to hear, '*Baigan lo aur ghusa dena!*' Shove a brinjal inside!

'The other girls laugh when one of their own gets beaten,' said Priya. '"Give her a few more!" they call out. "She's stealing our livelihood!"'

Although Priya bristled at having to dispense hafta, she never dwelt on it. It was preferable to the alternative.

A sex worker who couldn't afford hafta would be asked to pay the twelve hundred rupee fine for solicitation, even if she hadn't been soliciting at the time. If she argued that she hadn't fifty rupees, how could she possibly have twelve hundred, she would be told, 'Then suck it.' If she refused, she would be arrested. In jail, if she asked for a drink of water, she would be told, 'drink your urine.' If she started her menstrual cycle, she would have to tear a piece of her dupatta and place it in her underwear. The next day she would replace it with another piece of her dupatta.

Some of Priya's experiences were common enough in the line; she could trace them to the time she had moved to Bombay, half a dozen years earlier. But that summer, a new swagger and toughness was visible in the demeanour of even the ordinary constable on the street. That year, the excesses of the city police would include illegal detentions, extortion and torture, and the number of complaints registered against them, according to the National Crime Records Bureau, would be a staggering 26.6 for every 100 policemen. I assumed this number represented a fraction of complaints, since many victims would have been too afraid to file complaints against the police *to* the police, while others would have attempted to and met with resistance.

In their own way, though, even the police were victims of the new law. They were overworked—in the latter half of August alone they conducted raids in hundreds of dance bars and arrested two hundred people. This ratcheted up the work stress they already suffered which, according to documents obtained under the Right to Information Act, caused the death of one policeperson every forty-eight hours. And in their new role as aggressors, the police lost plenty of goodwill, and therefore informers, which affected the quality and speed of their work.

But all of this was fine print, of course, of use only to people like me. For Leela and Priya this information, even if they had access to it, meant nothing.

With these thoughts in mind, I got up to leave. And although I knew well I would be rebuffed, I couldn't help myself. If there's anything I can do, I said to Priya. Priya nodded briskly. 'Move out of the way,' she said, gesturing at the unfinished card game.

3

'If anything happens, run like Sita should have run from Ravan!'

Apsara wanted to seek the advice of a tantric. 'When will Goddess Lakshmi visit?' she moaned.

'When you start earning your own money,' snapped Leela. 'Go to a tantric, go to many, many tantrics. But fuck fortune; ask the tantric when you'll return to Meerut.'

'You don't want me to be happy.'

'Manohar didn't want you to be happy. I just want you to shut up.'

'Shettyji was such a good man. What were you drinking you let him go?'

'He let me go mummy, you know that. There's no one behind me now; no fighter. I'm alone. So let it be.'

'You're playing double games with me.'

'Please keep quiet.'

'Quiet! If I stay quiet a minute longer my head will burst into flames!'

'Then go for a walk.'

'Go for a walk, hahn Leela? No atta, no oil, fridge empty, stomach empty, *tijori* so empty a bird could lay eggs in it for sure—what for will I go for a walk? To walk under a car?'

This was a new era. Only a month earlier, before the loss of their livelihood, Apsara's only response to Leela's jibes would have been tears and an invocation to God to rescue her from this life.

But Apsara was no longer beholden to Leela—Leela barely paid her own way.

Their unresolved anger and distrust of each other peaked into paranoia. Each was convinced the other was hiding money from her.

'I came here for you,' Apsara screamed at Leela one morning. 'Why?' responded Leela calmly. 'All you do is eat.'

'Why? You're asking why! My daughter-in-law bought for me a car, a cooler, a washing machine,' ranted Apsara. 'You hear that, Leela madam? And she doesn't step out of the house without my permission, not even to take water from the well, even then she covers her face so well brought-up she is and so careful we are to protect our good name. But you, you have failed us! You are nothing but a tablawali! A mujrawali! A Bombay girl! You are a daring Bombay girl!'

Priya needed money too. The auto-rickshaw bijniss with Tinkoo was not working out for her. Dhanda is for other people, she explained to Leela, not for me, not for you. 'Right or wrong?'

Leela wanted to help, of course she did, but all the money she thought she had, '*gayab ho gaya*', vanished. Leela checked everywhere. The *Hanuman Chalisa* and all her handbags; over and over again, as though they contained hidden spaces that would with patience and in time reveal themselves to her. Then under the mattress, inside every shoe, between the pages of a *Femina* magazine she had 'borrowed' from Welcome, Good Looks. But luck had parted ways with Leela and her persistence was in vain. She had to refuse Priya and Priya sulked. '*Kya* yaar!' she grumbled, monopolizing the bed, drinking rum straight from the bottle. Apsara drank endless cups of tea. Rum, tea, rum, tea, tea, rum. Characteristically brushing aside Leela's feelings like her distress was less than theirs, Apsara and Priya bonded over their misfortune.

Tinkoo hadn't grown up in Bombay to let an opportunity, even one imagined, slip by. 'Accha, if you find your thousands,' he said to Leela with a confidential smile, 'why not throw a few notes my way? Priya and I want to start a bijniss in Surat. You know Surat, my hometown. There's huge demand for chhoti-chhoti*sis* among those dhokla-theplawalas.' He paused for effect. 'And don't we want Priya to retire from bijniss full-time?'

Leela walked away. 'Three hundred,' Tinkoo called out after her. 'That's our dream. Three hundred of the best little girls.'

He grinned, 'Three is my lucky number. I put the two zeroes in for my hero, James Bond.'

Leela's economic deterioration was immediate and clear. The cooler had been switched off; the television was now a foot stool. Apsara roasted chapattis for every meal, she was careful rolling the dough, maintaining uniformity of size— anything could set Leela off, she cursed. She dispensed each meal grimly.

Oh, those days of hotil-style khana and chilled beer, of endless boxes of cigarettes and bottomless cups of chai. Some days Leela had only to think of the food she had once ordered, of the frivolities she had enjoyed, to savour them once more, 'free *mein'*.

Despite her reduced circumstances, circumstances she had done nothing to bring upon herself, Leela reacted to my offerings of food the way she reacted to my offers of help.

I wanted to lend her money to tide her over until she found a job; she refused. I slipped some into her wallet when she wasn't looking; she clucked a reprimand and slipped it right back in my bag. I said I would introduce her to an NGO that might employ her as a peer educator. The money wouldn't be much, I warned, around three thousand rupees a month, but it was something.

'Three thousand!' cried Leela. 'What will I do with three thousand? Better I save my energy.' She recalled the bar girls' union—its founder would soon be charged with misappropriation of funds—'These NGOs are all the same I tell you. They fire over the shoulders of girls like us!'

When I asked Leela what she thought her alternatives were she answered, 'Don't worry *na*, things will work out.'

Leela was weeks away from returning to the start position on the game board of her life in Bombay. How could she stay so calm?

And yet, why was I surprised? Leela was unflappable. She behaved no differently when she learnt the results of her HIV test. Despite her promise to me, a promise I hadn't prompted, she refused to reveal what the doctor had said to her.

What did he say? Are you okay? I asked.

The first time Leela smiled as though to say, 'Of course, why wouldn't I be?'

Another time she said, 'Life is no game, just you remember that.'

Leela said no more, not to me, not even to Priya.

So I stopped asking and instead sought answers in how she coped.

Leela slept a great deal.

She listened to a borrowed radio.

She dreamt of gaon. 'I returned to my village last night,' she said. 'Everyone was there. My family, the friends I wished I had. Even the police, those ghoda maderchods, were standing around. But they didn't welcome me, they didn't celebrate my success. They did nothing, because they didn't see me. I walked through my house, they walked past me, I walked through the cantonment, they walked through me. I sat under a neem tree and cried and cried, and with my tears fell the leaves of all the trees around me. But no one consoled me. When I woke up I was crying, but then I stopped. What to cry for? I am invisible.'

She told jokes. 'Have you heard the one about Amitabh Bachchan and his answering machine?' No, I replied. 'What about the one in which the husband says to his wife, "You've become very fat", and she replies, "But I'm pregnant!"?' I shook my head. Leela sighed. Pity. It was zabardast, the funniest joke she had ever heard. If only I knew it, how much I would laugh, how we would laugh together.

'Jokes,' sneered Apsara. 'Is this the time for jokes?'

Priya mused, 'A kustomer was crazy for my attention. Finally he said, "Do you want to hear a good joke?" "No," I replied. "Why so?" he said. "Don't you like to laugh?"'

'I do like to laugh,' she told Apsara firmly. 'How I wish I had listened when kustomer had wanted to make me laugh.'

Priya gave up attempting to run a separate household. She moved in with Leela and Apsara, bringing with her complaints, clothes and a chatai. I assumed she had skipped out on her rent because she warned me to say 'Priya *gayi* gaon' to anyone who came asking.

༺

A few weeks later, I had a missed call. When I called back it was Paanwala Shyam who answered, for he also manned a PCO booth beside his paan stall below Leela's flat. When I asked who it was, he replied, 'Leela *ki* mummy.'

'Such a selfish girl,' Apsara started off. 'Just like my mother-in-law, no concern for others. Here I am; I've come all the way from Meerut having left behind my husband and sons, only because she begged, "Please give me company, mummy, I'll take care of you, God promise. I'll give you whatever you want to eat." And now without any notice she has left! Did she once ask herself—what people will say? How will mummy cope?'

What do you mean? I asked. Is Leela missing?

'I have varicose veins so big-big purple like baingan. I can't even walk. Where am I supposed to go looking for this girl, the burden, the burden that she is! Oh, it's true what they say! Boys love mummy most. They worship their mummy like a devi. But girls like Leela! No husband, no children, no shame. She has made me fall in the eyes of God!'

Does Priya know where she went?

'And all day, all time, stories; "Manohar did this, Manohar did that." *Badnami*! Manohar was so pious man, every weekend he would wash dishes at our gurdwara. And she says the police did ganda kaam with her. What ganda kaam? They were my mister's closest friends! Why, come Diwali time, inspector sahib would send such a big box of burfi! I haven't eaten mithai in God knows how many months! I've forgotten what meetha tastes like!

Oh, even small-small joys have been snatched from me! Why? Why, God, what sins did I commit in my past life? Why stuff my mouth with this most bitter taste of misfortune?'

Apsara, what about Priya? And Tinkoo?

'You're a very smart girl! Yes, you're right. That little slut has run off with Tinkoo.' She started to wail, 'My girl has run off with a pimp! Have you heard? Everyone, listen, listen: my girl has run off with a dalal! Hey bhagwan, bhagwan *bachao*, a dalal has kidnapped my angel.'

I phoned Priya. Tinkoo answered for her because Priya was 'too much busy'.

Doing what? I wondered, exasperated. She was no longer in rickshaw bijniss.

'Leela is all right,' Tinkoo said to me. 'Not to worry.'

So where is she?

'In lodge bijniss,' he said casually. I imagined him flicking.

What's lodge bijniss?

'Lodge-bijniss-means-lodge-bijniss,' Tinkoo replied, sounding taken aback. 'Why to worry?'

Because she's missing, I said.

'Missing? No, not missing at all. She's in lodge bijniss I just told, *na*?'

I raised my voice. Tinkoo, what do you mean by lodge bijniss?

'Be calm, Soniaji,' he sighed. 'No need for party-like excitement. See if you want, you come to Mira Road. I'll show you what is lodge bijniss, I'll show you to Leela, I'll show you nothing to worry. Happy? Tension free?'

I wondered if Tinkoo knew what he was talking about. Leela had never liked him and he seemed to me an unlikely confidant. But he was the only one of her small circle who had offered to help me find her and for this kindness I was grateful. So I took him up on his offer and we agreed to meet.

∽

The following evening, I stood outside Mira Road station, my cellphone in hand, to make sure I wouldn't miss Tinkoo. I needn't have worried. He liked to make an entrance.

Tinkoo zoomed up on a black motorcycle with an adrenaline-pumped roar and an explosion of exhaust fumes. His leather pants, half-open white shirt, tail flapping in the wind, and black hairband mirrored the current trend among young Bollywood actors, completing the picture he wished to present. Before he could put forward the suggestion I knew was on his lips, I quickly cut in. I'll follow you in an auto, I said, hoping he would take my rebuff as my attempt not to inconvenience him. But of course he knew it for what it was and offering me a mocking smile Tinkoo revved up and zipped off, zigzagging between taxis and trucks, almost running down a cyclist transporting baby parrots in individual cages.

Bombay is crammed with lodges and driving by in an auto-rickshaw I passed more than half a dozen. A lodge is most often a decrepit building, licked clean of paint and riddled with scars, scribbles and paan stains; stinking of urine. Sometimes known as a 'chadar *badal*', change the sheet, for only the top sheet was ever changed before a room was rented out again, a lodge was always named after a desirable quality: Happy Lodge, Lucky Lodge, Sweet Sleep Lodge. It charged scarcely a fee, because it offered no services and insisted on no rules. A sex worker I knew was drugged by a customer and when she regained conscious-ness found that she had been robbed of her wallet and cellphone. Another girl, I was told by her sister, had her tongue and nipples sliced off. Her customer removed the drawstring from her salwar and tied it around her neck, strangling her to death.

So the news that Leela had started working from a lodge signalled to me that she was desperate—willing to put her life in danger to make ends meet. As we passed one seedy lodge after another, my worry found traction and grew.

At our destination, I followed Tinkoo up long flights of stairs; the walls on either side so narrow, they appeared to want to close in on us. On the third floor, in a low-ceilinged room sat an elderly man on a plastic garden chair before a plastic garden table, his face all but hidden by a baseball cap. He did not look up from his newspaper when he asked, 'How much time?'

He did not look up, Tinkoo later said, because he was God-fearing and doing this because he had to, but he was so ashamed, he told his family he worked as a peon in a shoe factory, and he was so ashamed, he had sworn never to look customers in the eye.

'We've come for someone; Leela is her name,' Tinkoo said. 'She has a booking in Room 7.'

'Three hundred and fifty,' replied the man, his eyes still averted. 'Booking, no booking.'

I handed over the money.

Tinkoo laughed, 'Don't spend it on girls, uncle. Save some for your daughter's school fees!'

Tinkoo led the way up another flight of stairs and then through a poky, ill-lit corridor. In a corner was a vending machine manned by a boy humming along to music on his cellphone.

Walking up to a door marked '7' in white paint, Tinkoo rapped twice.

'Leela,' he called out, 'Tinkoo bhai here.'

'Leela?' he raised his voice, 'Tinkoo bhai. And Soniaji is with me.'

Confronted with silence Tinkoo tried the handle of the door. It opened easily, revealing a semi-dark room that cloyed with rum. Tinkoo's shoes crunched down on shards of glass. The bed was undone.

'She's not here,' he shrugged. 'And some *bevda*,' he sniffed, 'will not find his way home.'

What made you think she would be here? I asked.

'She's been renting this room for some time. You didn't know?' He bared his teeth. 'I thought you were sisters.'

For how long? I asked.

'A few weeks. I don't know exact. Life had become difficult for her, you know that. She wanted to earn enough to leave, to go someplace she could make money in peace; that also you know. Dubai probably she had in mind—all these girls have the same dream, it's no secret! It used to be "Bombay meri jaan". Now it's "Dubai meri jaan"! She would bring kustomers back here.'

A pair of jeans I recognized as Leela's hung from the back of a chair. Had she moved in?

Tinkoo nodded. 'Cigrit?'

I shook my head.

'You know that Apsaraji,' he continued, lighting himself a collapsed bit of Gold Flake. 'She could drive anyone crazy. Leela thinks Apsara stole from her. Otherwise, she said, where it went so quickly? How they fought! Like WWF wrestlers! If only I could have thrown some kachhas on them and pushed them into an *akhada*, what riches I would have made!'

I peeped into the bathroom. It was filthy. It stank of urine. A part of the floor had peeled back to reveal a layer of cement, chipped and cracked.

Tinkoo called out, 'Take a look at this.'

He pointed to the tube light above the bed. 'That's where they place the camera,' he said. 'For films. What films? Not *Heer Ranjha*! It points direct on bed, see. There should be another one, on top of the window, for a panoramic view. Sometimes the girls know what's going on and they go along with it. What choice do they have? They say, "If you give me a cut, then okay." But mostly it's done quietly. Someone hires the room for a half hour, he sets up his camera; when he returns to the room a week later he's set. He has enough maal for ten films. He makes a thousand DVDs, sells them for fifty rupees outside the station. If he's feeling generous he later puts it on the Internet for everyone to enjoy free *mein*. It's a booming bijniss I tell you. In fact, I'm considering it myself.'

Maybe she's out with a customer, I said.

Tinkoo shrugged. 'It doesn't seem to me that this room has been used for some days. What kustomer can afford a woman for so long? No. She probably couldn't pay her last bill and so she must have run, see how she left her clothes behind? So fast she must have run! By the way, you should know this, I'm on Yahoo. You know Yahoo? So for me getting into this bijniss won't be a problem. Because I have an email, as I said. All I need is someone to invest in me, to believe in me. A few thousand, if someone has, that would be okay. Why a few thousand? Even if one thousand someone has, anyone, doesn't have to be a friend of mine, can be a friend of a friend of mine, say a friend of Leela's . . . Now if a friend of Leela's were to offer me a thousand rupees towards my bijniss that would be okay with me.'

We left the lodge and I hailed another auto-rickshaw, following Tinkoo as he drove to Night Lovers. The board outside indicated that it was still closed and the red-bearded security guard who had, until so recently, impressed me with his fierce demeanour, now sat back on a chair with his legs propped against the gate, his expression one of boredom.

'Sahib gaon *gaye*,' he said.

ॐ

We returned to Leela's street. It was the start of the evening and her neighbours had thrown open their windows and cracked open their doors to welcome the cool air. On the broken concrete children made do: teenagers played cricket, boys tossed around a football, girls raced about on identical pink bicycles, the littlest ones stuck together, chattering of tea parties, kitty parties, their weddings. Their collective shouts and open laughter mingled with the evening's smells—peanuts roasting on a charcoal fire, a half-dozen buffaloes harrumphing towards their *tabela*, depositing loads of grassy manure on their way.

We stopped by all the people Leela knew—Paanwala Shyam, Aftab her tailor friend, even her immediate neighbours, bar dancers, all of whom appeared wan and distracted, and given their circumstances, understandably uninterested in our questions.

No one knew where she was.

Finally, I phoned Baby. 'I've changed NGOs,' Baby said distantly. 'And you know Leela. She never keeps in touch.'

I felt like I had run out of options. And I was worried too that Tinkoo would want to leave to be with Priya.

But he was enthusiastic to continue searching with me.

'Priya has attitude,' he confided. 'Arre, if you have to do dhanda, do dhanda. You can't be having your nose in the air saying "don't put it here, don't put it there; I'm not that sort of girls". Okay fine, you look like Aishwarya Rai. But you're not married to Abhishek Bachchan, you're married to dhanda. So why say "*is* kaam *mein* izzat *nahin hai*"? There is no dignity in such work. Did you get into it for your izzat or for your survival? If you want izzat, madam, open your own brothel. Otherwise, keep your legs open.'

Priya has retired? I tried to confirm. From rickshaw business?

'What can I say?' sighed Tinkoo. 'This is the problem with these girls. Commitment? Zero per cent! As soon as Priya made a bit of money, she moved into my flat, it's not even my flat mind you, it's my friend's, but there she was making herself as comfortable as a queen. Now my friend wants us to leave because he says Priya makes his woman uncomfortable with her big-big eyes and showy talk. And money gets spent does it not? Already I have to do "*do* number *ka* kaam" to feed us. I'm confused, Soniaji. I thought a dalal was supposed to make money from his woman. But it seems like I'm going to be making money *for* my woman.'

I smiled. Of course, Priya had Tinkoo wrapped around her little finger. How could she not? And Tinkoo, I suspected, enjoyed the attention.

I wondered if he thought of it as affection.

Well, there's nowhere else I can think of to look, I said to him in a friendly voice. Let's go up to Leela's and wait.

'Why?' Tinkoo shook his head. 'Once Apsaraji starts her *ghitar-pitar—khit-khit* in front of you, *ghus-pus* behind your back—you will run away too and then I will have to look for Leela *and* for you! Leave her alone. You know what, we should go to Aksa.'

But that's hours away. Why would she go there? I asked, worried.

'Because she's desperate. Do you not see how it is with these women? Before, they had balance, meaning money, but they had no brains. And now Leela has no balance, she has found her brains and realizes that without money she cannot survive Bombay city.'

I wondered if he was right about Aksa. Leela had taken me there a few months ago. She wanted me to see what happened to women who couldn't leave the line.

I told Tinkoo about that evening.

An unexpected downpour had forced us to take shelter in the auto-rickshaw that had driven us over from Malad station. Passing time, we spoke of many things, among them of Leela's desire to move someplace new.

'Bahar *ka* life bahut achha *hai*,' she had sighed. Life abroad is good.

Where do you want to go? I asked.

Anyplace. Lundun sounded good; there were many Indians there, she had heard. 'But how to reach?' The last time she had travelled anywhere far she had been thirteen. And Lundun was far, far away. God knows how many planes, trains and cars would do the trick! Who would she go to if something terrible happened? And what of the cold? She had heard the rain fell like stones. And she had no sweaters. If she did find something suitable in Mira Road for sure it would be unsuitable for Lundun. People would point. And laugh! Why would she go to Lundun to be laughed at? Might as well stay home.

Leela sighed. Gaon was best. Everyone dreams of returning to their village towards the end of their life. And in one's dreams the village is beautiful. There are flowers everywhere, the trees are laden with fruit. Neighbours are kind, the police mind their bijniss not yours. In Leela's dream, she has plenty of friends, and oh, how they admire her, how they fight for her attention! And to return to this paradise a success! Laden with jewellery, with two-two bags of new clothes and shoes and utensils, with presents for everyone, full of stories that would make even the panchayat's eyes pop! That was her dream. But would it come true?

You're not even halfway through your life, I said lightly.

'You think so?'

Leela's shrug seemed to say: maybe you're right. Maybe you're not.

When the rain died down I paid the auto driver, and Leela and I began to walk across the beach.

Wild grey waves roared bullishly at us and the wind struck our faces sharp, salty and cold. We reached a cloister of palm trees and suddenly we were walking on a carpet of used condoms, and where there weren't condoms there were condom packets and elsewhere were beer bottles and pornographic material, even bed sheets mangled by the wind.

'A brothel has a madam,' said Leela. 'The street is full with public. But Aksa? Who cares for Aksa? Anything goes because nobody cares.'

I knew what she meant about Aksa's isolation. It was considered so out of the way people from other parts of Bombay went there on vacation, to enjoy the beach and eat seafood. Those with money stayed at 'The Resort', a beachfront hotel popular with young middle-class families. But all the way to The Resort were clusters of *wadis*, or villages, with neat houses and front gardens bursting with flowers, with domesticated hens, goats, cats and dogs. Contrary to the rural idyll they projected, some of these villages made their money from brothels, the majority of which functioned out of homes. Even if the guests at The Resort were unaware of this, they couldn't possibly miss the sex workers that lined the road to their hotel—they clustered at the bus stop in their bindis and bangles; they refused to let a man pass without comment. The ones on the beach were forthright. 'Won't you have some fun with me?' they would pout, patting a spot beside them.

That afternoon, right outside The Resort, Leela introduced me to two sex workers she was acquainted with. Soma was short and fat with bristly black hair on her cheeks. She greeted Leela cheerfully and continued to dig through her stubby fingernails for food. Sangeeta wore a tough expression and had half a dozen teeth. Nodding at Leela she pointed to a large, puffy scrape on the side of her face.

'She was having an affair with my boyfriend,' she grumbled. 'I gave her one jhap. She cut me.'

'Who? Soma?' Leela asked, confused.

Sangeeta looked at her as though she was stupid.

'Why would Soma sleep with my boyfriend?'

'She wouldn't,' Leela said immediately. 'Of course she wouldn't.'

'We are not that close I would share my mister like he was a vada-pav. My best friend Anita slept with him. You know Anita?'

Leela and I nodded vigorously. It was an 'Indian' nod. We could have meant 'yes, I know Anita', 'no, I don't' or 'please explain'.

I leaned in. The liquid appearance of Sangeeta's scrape suggested it was still fresh. She must be in pain, I thought. But before I could say anything else, we were interrupted by an elderly man reeking of drink and clutching awkwardly at his southward-heading dhoti. Thrusting a fifty rupee note into Sangeeta's hand he mumbled, 'Come on.'

'*Hat!*' growled Sangeeta. 'Can't you see I'm busy? That I have guests!' She turned to me, aggrieved. 'See this dirty grandfather? This is the sort of kustomer I get, curse my luck.' She listed the other undesirables. 'Bhangi, Musalman, *hamali*, jhaduwala, Chamar, Kumbar, Kadiya, helper, *havaldar*, inspector, harami saale. Whatever their caste, they are all like this motherfucker. Animals!'

The man offered us a confused grin; he thought we were playing with him. Obviously, we were there to work. Then why wouldn't we?

He repeated his request with an oily smacking of his lips. 'Chal *na*,' he implored.

Sangeeta struck his hand. 'Teri ma *ki*! Ask me once more and I swear I'll hit you!'

'Hit me,' he cajoled hoarsely.

'Now I'll show you!' Sangeeta said. 'You miserable cunt!' She looked this way and that, apparently for some sort of weapon, and then, as quickly, changed her mind. Throwing me a shifty glance, she snatched the fifty rupee note out of the man's hand and stuffed it into her sari blouse. There was already a cellphone in there, along with some money, a packet of gutka and a photograph.

The man grinned with relief and lifting his hand in farewell, scurried down the path to Sangeeta's designated spot. As Sangeeta stood up to follow, Leela said, 'Bye bye. And don't forget to wear a condom!'

'You sound like that cunt I used to work for,' Sangeeta sniffed. 'She'd say, "Sister, don't forget condom!" But she charged me twenty-five rupees for a condom, even though she got them for free. So I would use it. And then I would wash it and use it again, and then again, and then one more time. Twenty-five times! Why did I bother? Was there a single kustomer who didn't bite holes through a condom he wore?'

Your madam? I confirmed.

Sangeeta nodded. 'She made me pay to stand on the road. The public road. The whore! Okay, now I'm going. Listen,' she turned to Leela, 'if I were you I would go too and take your friend with you. Otherwise people will think you're working and they will ask, "How much?" Men over here have a dirty way of looking at women. Even good women aren't safe.'

'We'll be fine,' Leela said, patting her shoulder. 'Go on and do your bijniss, don't worry about us. You take care of yourself.'

ᖆᕼ

'That old whore was right,' said Tinkoo. 'Aksa's kustomers are animals. But are the women of Aksa any better? Their two legs are two too many!'

Tinkoo explained that shortly before she disappeared, Leela had mentioned Aunty, a prominent Aksa madam many bar dancers had begun working with for her reputation. Aunty, they said, was ancient, like Aksa, and therefore reliable. She liked pretty women. She was no 'gaal *pe* blade *dalnewali*'—she didn't mark their faces with a blade like some madams did, to show ownership, to keep her girls terrified and close. And she didn't allow customers to cut them either. She was a fine 'bijnissman' and was rightfully taking advantage of the boom in the 'randi bazaar' by offering bar dancers 50 per cent of their day's take. 'Of course,' mused Tinkoo, 'once the girls lose their looks, she won't give them 50 per cent, she won't even give them ten. But look how she's pulling them in now! Like a politician!'

He was impressed. Other people had all the good ideas!

Aunty was rich, Tinkoo continued. 'Wait till you see where she lives. You'll go mad.'

What's her name? I asked.

'Aunty.'

That can't be her name, I said. That's like calling someone Mr.

Tinkoo grinned at me. 'All right, call her Salma. Or Sangeeta. Call her whatever you like. But mind me Soniaji, she will answer only to Aunty.'

The following day I met Tinkoo outside The Resort in Aksa. He was dressed like a rap star—how he thought a rap star might look. He wore sunglasses, a stringy black vest, baggy black jeans and an alphabet chain that said 'handsome'. He asked me to follow him and so we drove awhile, down quiet roads, the sea on one side, gently swaying coconut trees on the other. After about twenty minutes he stopped in front of an imposing wooden gate, its great height preventing us from looking over. Turning to me he slid off his sunglasses and said, 'You're a *doctorni*.'

Really? I retorted.

'Yes,' he said sternly. 'Or a kustomer. Which do you prefer?'

Doctorni, I had to admit.

Tinkoo parked his motorcycle and pushed his way through the gate. I followed into a watercolour. In front of us stood six small cottages—'for sex,' Tinkoo unnecessarily informed me. The cottages had thatched roofs and brick walls and they were tapestried with knotted vines and brilliantly coloured flowers.

Flowers grew everywhere, even beneath my feet, even popping out of ditches like the ditches were vases. There was a picturesque well and by its side a blue bucket tied to a rope. In the background, the sea was a blinding silver light.

I couldn't help but contrast this magical location with Gazala's brothel in Kamatipura. I doubt her hijras cared. Their burdens wouldn't ease. But Aunty's property was so stunning, so well tended to, it made me curious about who she was: what kind of woman would on the one hand nurture beauty and on the other help ravage it?

I didn't have to wonder long. Tinkoo was pointing into the near distance, where an older woman was strolling beside a sprite of a man clutching a scythe. As she pointed first here and then there, the man bent down and rustled through the undergrowth, repeatedly emerging with a fallen coconut. When the woman spotted us, she strolled over with a smile.

Gazala's curious appearance had nothing on Aunty. She was a pixie with pale, deeply wrinkled skin and a crew cut the colour of ripe cherries. Although she must have been around fifty, she dressed somewhat like a Cabbage Patch Kid in lime green shorts, a flimsy vest in a similar colour and pink slippers from which the dye had bled, turning the soles of her feet, I would later note, a delectable candyfloss.

Aunty said, 'Ai hensum.' She leaned on her toes to kiss Tinkoo on the cheek like she was welcoming him to a tea party. Lowering her voice, she said, 'So, who is this one you've brought and what she wants?'

Tinkoo kissed her back, 'Hello Aunty,' he replied. 'She's a doctorni.'

Aunty pecked Tinkoo's other cheek, 'But does she know?'

'Of course! She knows everything.'

Aunty grabbed my hand in a claw-like grip, 'My dear girl,' she said, still speaking English in an accent I couldn't place. 'Business is so bad I have nothing to offer you—not a cup of tea, not coconut water. If only you had come a few months earlier you would have seen how I really live—in what style! I had a driver! A cook! A peon! One person just to cut my *bhaji*! But now they've all gone and do you know where?'

Clearly no further introduction was required of me.

'When I first hired those fucks,' Aunty went on, directing me towards one of the cottages, 'all they knew was to stand under a coconut tree and wait for coconuts to fall into their hands. Then one fuck asked, "Aunty, how much do you charge?" and another fuck said, "Aunty tell no, what's the best way to increase revenue?" and so I taught them everything I knew, thinking it would be useful for me to have people who understood the business. But how did they thank me? One fuck opened a brothel on my right, the other on my left. One fuck offers free beers with his fucks, the other says, "I don't care how many women you bring in as long as the door shuts behind you." So now Aksa is full of brothels and no one comes to Aunty.'

We seated ourselves cross-legged on the porch. Aunty's shorts hiked all the way up her bony hips. She had forgotten underwear.

Tinkoo was fascinated.

When could I ask of Leela?

Aunty had her own plans. She plucked a joint out of her bra and foraging in her back pockets retrieved a lighter. Lighting the joint, she took a puff. She exhaled. And she started to cry. 'I fucked myself,' she sobbed. 'How I fucked myself.'

I was startled. I looked over at Tinkoo, wanting to follow his cue.

He was unperturbed. 'Tell everything Aunty,' he encouraged. 'Soniaji is my sister.'

Aunty handed the joint to Tinkoo, who grabbed it eagerly. 'What you've missed, dear girl,' she said. Tears continued to roll down her face. I held out my hand to comfort her. Aunty grabbed it and started massaging my fingers with hard circular movements.

'This place,' she said, wiping her face on her t-shirt, kneading away, 'was exact like Kamatipura. Exact! So many people fucking, forty girls I had at one time and they weren't darky and ugly as they all seem to be these days, but beautiful, like in the movies, the black and white movies mind you, not the masala nonsense of today. Each one of them earned at least ten thousand rupees a night. Now all the girls are the same. Dark darky ducklings. What is their purpose? Does a man want to eat *rajma* rice outside his home, when at home all he gets is rajma rice, rajma rice and some more rajma rice?'

I shook my head.

'But the moment a beautiful girl wants to work for me one darky randi *log* or another, getting scare of the competition, invades my property and chases her away. "The police will arrest you! If they catch you with a condom, they will put you in jail!" What condom? Most of these girls have never seen a condom! Give them a condom, they will fill it with water and play balloon-balloon. A man wants a beautiful woman. Not someone who reminds him of his wife! Right or wrong? These randis will get two rupees if they get paid at all!'

I'm looking for a friend of mine, I said, withdrawing my hand. I was wondering if she was here. Her name is Leela.

'Leela?' Aunty said thoughtfully. 'Darky? Pretty?'

Pretty, I said.

I was suddenly flooded with sadness.

Aunty's face softened. 'Poor pretty. Must be somewhere, getting fucked up the backside.'

She's my height, I said. She has long hair, till here. I indicated.

Her eyes are black, but she often wears contact lenses.

'I wonder sometimes if it isn't best to be darky,' said Aunty. 'The pretty ones? No peace. Now, dear, look at me, looking at me now, would you say I was once pretty?'

Yes, I sighed.

'Exact!' agreed Aunty with enthusiasm. Her tears had dried quickly. 'I get it from my father's side. Anglo-Indians, you know. So fair-fair and light-eyed too. High-class! But it isn't enough to have looks, my dear; head sense means something too. I made a mistake. I married a man beneath my station. He owned a bar near Marine Drive. A bar and well, let's be frank, he had a side business with women. Mind you, he loved me to death. I had no work in the house other than picking up the phone. "Aunty dear," he would say, "I don't want you to darky your hands, let the servants do everything." But then he died and his business partner, fuck him twice, he stole all of his money, and I was left with nothing but this house.'

'Then what, Aunty?' Tinkoo hustled, unwilling to relinquish the joint.

'Then what means what? I had no choice but to stand at the door waiting for someone to approach me. That first time I waited for days. Then finally people understood—this is what she does. A man came, he finished, he rolled to one side and he asked, "How much?" I didn't know the answer! I said, "Whatever makes you happy." Another time a man lived with me for fifteen days. He ate, drank and fed me too. When he left he gave me nine rupees.'

'One day Aunty thought, "Why should I do this when I can make money off other women doing it?"'

'Exact,' said Aunty.

'Soon Aunty became famous.'

'I don't know why kustomers liked me,' she preened. 'But they did! They would say, "Madam, I like how you speak, what you say, even how you say it." I would reply, "Fine, my dear boy, but what of my girls? What of my rooms? Do you like them?" And they would blush like little children, "We like you, that's all we know!" Remember, my dear, kustomers don't belong to you or to me. They are free to do what they want with their money and with their cocks. And if, despite that freedom, they come back to you and say, "I like you!" it's an achievement. It's like winning a prize! Ah prizes . . . That reminds me, my dear, did you know that when I was in school I won first prize in a singing-song competition? Can you believe it? Me!'

How nice, I said. What about Leela? You know, the bar dancer?

'Now, of course, my dear, there are more polis than kustomers who come to dip their cocko into my girls. Those that don't come for sex, come for cash. Mind you,' Aunty shrugged, 'I don't mind paying hafta. After all, the polis have to eat too. Some fuckers pay the polis to protect them from kustomers but I have my methods, I don't need no polis-wolis. If a man has sex with one of my girls and then refuses to pay, I say, "As you wish!" But the next time he comes by I'm standing at the gate with a mutton knife in my hand. I tell him, "This time, mister, you *will* leave something behind. So for your sake, make sure it's money."'

Tinkoo giggled, 'Aunty will cut them also, they know it!'

I was beginning to lose patience.

Tinkoo, I said, isn't there something you want to ask Aunty?

He was thoughtful. 'No,' he said frankly. 'Nothing.'

I glared at him.

'Oh yes! Leela! Aunty, do you know this girl, Leela? Has she been here?'

'You do go on, don't you,' Aunty said. 'Why do you ask?' She leaned forward eagerly. 'A kustomer wants her, is it? You are the go-between, is it?'

No, she's a friend.

'A friend called Leela,' Aunty mused. 'Hmmm. Okay, come with me.'

Aunty grabbed the joint from Tinkoo's hand and started walking towards one of the other cottages. She flung open the door and we heard a yelp and saw a man dive under the bed. The very young, very naked girl he had left behind sighed. '*Kya*, Aunty,' she said, languidly. She motioned at the joint between Aunty's fingers and Aunty leaned forward and stuck it into the girl's mouth. From under the bed came a small voice. 'Hello, Auntiji, can you please pass pant-shirt?'

Aunty dug through the bed sheets and obliged.

'Thank you.'

'How are you, my son?' Aunty said, peering under the bed.

'*Bahut badiya.*' Very good.

Aunty straightened up and turned to me, 'I noticed you have a camera. Would you like to take some photos?'

No! I said, stepping away, pulling at Tinkoo's arm.

And this isn't Leela.

'Of course, this isn't Leela. Her name is Poonam. Am I right, dear? Your name is Poonam?'

The girl nodded and looked away.

Then why are we here?

'This is not Leela,' said Aunty. 'I know that! I was being polite, my dear. I just wanted to show you around. Have you been to Aksa before? Really? Who would have thought? . . . Now what is your friend's name? Leela? Oh yes, now I remember. She was a lovely. So young. She was here for a couple of days and then she had a fight with one of her kustomers and left. I don't get involved, my dear. That is how I keep my sanity and my life. She said to me, "I'm going now," and I said, "Okay. But if anything happens, run like Sita should have run from Ravan!"'

Do you know where she went? I asked.

Aunty shook her head. 'A randi without options, where will she run?'

Thanking Aunty, I prodded Tinkoo out of the door.

4

'They showed me. They showed me all night'

The weeks passed and I continued to receive rambling calls from Apsara. Sometimes she demanded to know where I had hidden Leela, at other times she begged me to find her and bring her home. Tinkoo called as well, mostly to discuss his latest business plan.

Then one sunny afternoon, about three weeks after my visit to Aunty, I got a call from Baby.

'I met Leela!' she screamed excitedly.

Is she okay?

'Fine—on the outside! But come quickly. She's in Cheetah Camp and keeps threatening to leave. Sajida *apa* worries that if she does leave we'll lose her forever. She'll get picked up by a pimp or be funnelled into a brothel.'

Cheetah Camp? I thought. Where was that? And Sajida apa? Who was she?

I asked Baby for the address. 'What address?' she said. 'Just come to Cheetah Camp and ask for Sajida apa.'

I phoned Paanwala Shyam and left a message for Apsara and Priya. Then I went online to find out more. Cheetah Camp was a predominantly Muslim slum settlement of approximately 100,000 daily wage earners. It had a tumultuous history. The previous year, in 2004, an altercation between local Muslims and Hindus carrying out a temple procession had left twenty-three people injured.

'Every few days they catch a "terrorist" here,' a resident

complained in a newspaper report. 'This has given Cheetah Camp a bad name as a dangerous locality.'

As I got out of the auto-rickshaw and viewed the vast sprawl ahead of me, I realized why Baby had been unable to provide me with an address. Cheetah Camp was a settlement of small, even rooms separated by what seemed no more than a finger-width of space. Outside these rooms life was lived openly: daughters combed their mothers' hair, mothers bathed babies, and little children, their eyes wet with colds, their feet sloppy with mud, played in the sewer that zigzagged through the camp. The sewer was thick with flies that buzzed drill-like over hillocks of faeces.

Spinning wheels of dust raced through the air, and the air was as hot and smoky as a firecracker.

Although it was past conventional work hours, everyone was invested in a task—in domestic chores, prepping and cooking food in open-air stalls, manning shops that sold shanks of raw meat and eggs and fruit and sacks of lentils. These activities gave the camp a sharp, invigorating liveliness.

I had to ask several people the way to Sajida apa's, but she was well known and I was able to navigate the narrow lanes with steady ease.

Sajida apa's door was wide open and in the darkness, lit only by the blue light of an aquarium of shimmering, brightly coloured fish, sat Baby on a carpet, with a small, plump woman I guessed was Sajida apa. She appeared to be in her early sixties. Her white hair was pulled back in a bun, her light-brown eyes were lined with kohl and her squat, pink face was creased into deep lines. She was stroking a sewage-coloured kitten mewling with pleasure.

Baby jumped up and introduced me. Sajida apa nodded distractedly. 'I hope you like biryani,' she said. 'I would like you to stay for dinner.'

Baby lowered her voice. 'She has come for . . .' she inclined her head towards the adjoining room, which was demarcated by a thick pink curtain. 'We have some things we would like to discuss with her. Is there a hotil close by we can go to?'

Sajida apa raised an eyebrow. She looked Baby up and down. Baby was wearing a salwar kameez. She did the same to me. I was in my standard-issue reporter's outfit—a kurta and a comfortable pair of jeans.

'But the hotils here are full of men,' Sajida apa said. 'There is no separate ladies' section in this area. Do you want to sit open-faced, among men, in a hotil?'

'Of course not!' cried Baby. She offered an abashed smile. 'I'm mad. I should have come in a burkha.'

She turned to me. 'Fine then, the two of you chat. I will keep Sajida apa company.'

Sajida apa looked at me. 'I work in the local Mahila Mandal,' she said, referring to a social empowerment group. 'There are a lot of young Muslim girls in the bar line. I follow up on them. I try to stop them from destroying their future by offering them small jobs in beauty parlours, doing henna design. One of my girls came across your girl and told me about her.'

'Sajida apa and I are old friends,' explained Baby. 'That's why she called me.'

Sajida apa angled her face as though she was talking to the fish. 'Tell your girl,' she said, 'Tell her life is hard. There is no point making it harder on oneself. Even good girls, they get into trouble. A girl will spend her life preparing for marriage, learning how to please a man. She will do no wrong, and how will her husband repay her? With *talaq*. The number of talaqs in this locality, by God! What are our men up to? They marry, they have a child, two childs. If nothing changes then neither do they. But if they make money and move upwards in life, they just have to show the world, make a show for the world. And what better way than with a new wife? So they say talaq, talaq, talaq. *Zubaani* talaq! On the phone. SMS talaq! And they remarry. But do they have the decency to find a woman elsewhere? No! They marry in the same mohalla, again and again. They give us a bad name. As if we don't have enough problems! And this is with the good girls, mind you. The ones who don't deserve what comes to them.'

'As if the bar line is any better,' Baby said. 'In the bar line our name is mud. "The Mohameddans are the worst," people say. "They have dozens of children—ten, twelve, fifteen—and they can't afford to feed, clothe or educate them. So what do they do? Push their daughters into the bar line! Make them dance! And all the while they're paying for abba, ammi, bhai, behen. And they have babies, so many babies! More and more babies! And they change their name! From Imtiaz to Roshni! From Salma to Seema! Meena, Jyoti, Pinky, Tina!"'

'But there is truth in this,' sighed Sajida apa. 'We do these things, why lie? Why didn't we fight R.R. Patil like the Hindus did? So many of our girls are in this line, I cannot tell you, it's our greatest shame. But what's the alternative? If we don't educate our girls, school them well, what will they eat? How will they feed us? What will they do but seduce men for money? Anyway, we can talk of these things later. Your girl was having a bath, but she must be ready now.'

⌒

Leela was enveloped in what must have been one of Sajida apa's nightdresses. With her knees drawn up to her stomach and her eyes closed, with no make-up to obscure the innocence of her face, she looked as she was: a young girl. Her wet hair splashed across the pillow gave it a shadow of dampness, but I wondered if the dampness wasn't also of her tears. I thought she was asleep and so I perched gingerly on the edge of the bed, waiting for her.

'Where did you disappear?' Leela murmured. 'Why did you leave?'

I was startled.

'*Tumne toh dimag* out *kar diya*.' You drove me out of my mind.

'Wasn't that what you were going to say?' she laughed, snapping open her eyes.

I was so worried, I agreed.

She still has her sense of humour, I thought to myself with relief.

'Sajida apa is crazy,' Leela said. 'She has a name for each one of her fish, and before she goes to bed she kisses them through the glass, tata-bye bye! She calls them her jaans.'

She sounds crazy, I smiled.

'And since I've arrived she's been after me to learn cooking. When I said to her, "If I start cooking won't all the hotils go out of bijniss?" she insisted I attend a mehendi design class. Mehendi! Is that what she thinks I'm worth? Or does she presume that because I'm a barwali I'll take anything that's thrown my way? Kaam *nahin toh* mehendi *sahi?* No work, so mehendi? I'm a dancer, not a mehendiwali, not a *bawarchi*! Someone tell her that!'

You don't have to do anything you don't want to, I said.

'I'll sit on her cat!'

And you don't have to stay here, or with Apsara. We'll figure something out.

Leela mumbled into her pillow.

I can't hear you, I said.

'My brother is coming for me,' she repeated.

I thought you didn't care for your brothers.

'Speak with respect! He's my blood.'

I didn't mean it that way. I just thought you didn't get along. If you need a place to stay we'll find you one. You don't have to worry.

'I have a hundred places to stay; I don't need charity.'

It's not charity.

Leela turned her face away.

After a few minutes of silence, I stepped out. Sajida and Baby had thoughtfully moved their conversation and the kitten to the darkness of the stoop. I interrupted them to ask of Leela's brother.

When is he coming? I said.

Sajida apa looked up with a sigh. 'Is that what she told you?'

Isn't it true?

She shook her head. 'Her phone got stole and so she called home from the PCO booth. Her brother said, "Stay there, I'll reach in two days." But the day after, when I called to confirm what time his train would arrive, he said to me, "Don't mind, but can you keep Leela for a while? It's just that I started a new bijniss and if I bring home a sister who used to work in bars, I'll lose all my customers. My good name too." I told him what I thought of him—factory of shamelessness! But I couldn't tell Leela. What would I say, you tell? It's always the same with these girls—a horror film!'

She helped him start his business, I said. With her money.

'Don't take it personally,' Sajida shrugged. 'We should be grateful she had the sense to ask for help. She had no money, so she walked into one of our sister organizations in Khar and they notified me because of my experience with such girls. Otherwise, do you know what could have happened to her? A lost girl her age in small-small clothes walking up and down the road on her own, with nothing to say for herself but her name? I've heard of girls younger than her, ten years younger than her, kidnapped for doing exactly what she did, kidnapped, beaten and then sold into sex. You think she is in trouble, let me tell you she is lucky. Your girl is a lucky girl and you should tell her that.'

Baby sighed, 'She's right.'

'She's being a princess!' Sajida said, growing angry. 'What for is she sorry for herself? I can show you pictures, I have pictures of girls, how they were rescued. One was kept in a cage made for a dog! You can try, try all you want, I tell you. But you cannot change her ending.'

'Her ending is her own,' agreed Baby. 'She is responsible for it.'

I went back inside and sat beside Leela. Sajida doesn't want to tell you, I said. Your brother isn't coming for you.

'As if I don't know,' she whispered.
Let me help you.
'Don't you want to know where I went?'
If you want to tell me.
'To my favourite place.'
McDonald's, Lokhandwala?
She smiled.
What did you eat?
'Burger-fry,' she smiled weakly. 'And two Cokes.'
Did you find a toy?
'Yes, on the floor. Oh, but then I lost it. So sad.'
She was quiet for a moment.

∾

'I ate and ate and I stayed until it closed. Then I sat outside and thought through everything. So I have bad luck, I thought to myself. Bad luck is in my blood. It is true what they say—destiny is as strong as iron, it is tougher than steel; nothing can change what is written for you. Because even after I ran away from my father and mother, even when I did everything I could to make myself better, better than what they had tried so hard to make me, even then I couldn't change what was destined for me.

'I just sat there, like a fool.

'Then some girls came up to me. One of them asked why I was crying. I said, "That's my bijniss." The other one said, "If it's your bijniss, why are you alone, away from your family?" They asked if I was thirsty. When I said "yes" they shared a bottle of daru with me. And so I knew we were alike. We started drinking and I told them everything. Oh, how satisfying it was! They asked if I'd like to come along with them to work, to a disco called Magnus, in Khar. Do you know what a disco is?'

I think so, I said.

'No you don't. It's not what you think. It's not what you know. It looks like a disco, but it's really a brothel. Only men are allowed inside. All the girls are in half-half clothes. They dance and sit on the laps of men and put their tongues in their mouths. One of the girls said to me, "*Tum bhi nacho, nahin to hamari* insult *ho jayegi.*" If you don't dance, we'll feel insulted. What was it to me? I started dancing. I don't know what happened next but when I woke up it was morning. I was on the floor of someone's house and all my clothes had been removed from me.'

You should have called me, I said.

'Why? What had to happen would happen. Destiny, remember? And why for would I have gone home? To have Apsara call me a whore? No, I had no choice. I stayed with the girls, they became my gang. We went to Magnus every night. Then they started taking me to private parties in people's houses. I almost went to jail! One night I was with a police inspector when we heard a commotion—"*Bhago*, police! Randi chal hat!" It was a raid! But my policeman was a decent man. "Quick," he said, "jump into your clothes and get out through the bathroom window. Keep running and don't look back. I'll take care of this." How I laughed as I ran fast-fast like a thief! I felt like a Hindi film heroine running away from goonda-bhai *log*! I thought God was smiling down on me again.

'But then . . . Can girls live in peace? Huh! They turned on me, of course. It happened after a nanga naach. I had been told there would be "Navy", that I would have to take off my clothes. After Navy, kustomers decide who gets which girl and for how much. I was never more disgusted. Not with the men. What can one expect of men? With the girls! Many of them had come with their children; some appeared only a few weeks old. They placed their children in a corner and immediately started dancing. Next thing I saw they were taking off their clothes and performing in their underwears to *Main aayi hoon UP Bihar lootne.* They were roaming in their chaddis! Openly! Shamelessly! Their children were staring at them with their thumbs in their mouths, their milk bottles by their side. They were probably wondering, "What is mummy doing?" Why was I upset? I don't know. They weren't my children after all, and if their mothers didn't dance what would they put in their milk bottles? Blessings? But when we returned home that night I said to my friends, "No more. I don't want to see this any more." My gang was upset with me. They tried to . . .'

Baby was tapping on the wall. 'Leela?' she called out.

'Come in, Baby,' Leela said. 'Come in. What's the matter?'

Baby parted the curtain and, lowering her voice, said, 'Sajida apa is getting a little impatient. She wants to serve dinner.'

Tell her I'll be out soon, I said.

'Five times she has told me that she used *real* saffron and *real* cashew nuts and that if we don't eat quickly the biryani won't taste any good. Like *real* biryani.'

'Real biryani!' Leela snorted.

'Sorry,' Baby said apologetically. 'Sajida apa worries so much about her girls. I'm scared for her health. She may get a heart attack! Cooking is a good distraction, wouldn't you say? At least for Sajida apa. It takes her mind off the girls.'

'Also fish,' Leela quipped. 'Food and her fish.'

Five minutes, I said to Baby. Please?

Baby nodded sympathetically and went back out.

'They went crazy,' Leela continued. 'They took my refusal personally, as though by refusing to dance naked I was refusing their friendship. To my face they said "as you wish". But that night in Magnus they got me real drunk. So drunk I couldn't walk. I wanted to leave but they kept saying, "What's the hurry?" Finally, when all the other girls had left, when even the manager was collecting his thailis, they took me to the bathroom. They threw me against a wall and one of them took off her belt and started beating me. I had bought that belt for her from Linking Road, two days back. It was Tommy Hilfiger. Good brand! After they beat me they cleaned me up. Then they pushed me into their car. One of them said, "Have you met my brother? He's very *chikna*, very hensum. You want to be a good girl *na*? You don't want to do Navy no more *na*? He'll show you." We drove for a few minutes; we were still in Khar. They made me walk up to the fifth floor. Her brother was waiting for us. Him and his five friends. They showed me. They showed me all night. Then, when it was time for them to leave, they opened the door and kicked me down the stairs. No clothes, no chappals, nothing. Here, see.'

Leela reached into her pocket and, retrieving something, held it out for me.

It was a tooth.

I didn't understand.

She opened her mouth wide.

I stared at her palm.

'Don't start,' Leela warned gruffly.

I couldn't help the tears in my eyes. I looked up at her.

'This is why I didn't call you! Because I knew this would happen. I knew it! Let it be. I said, let it be! Call the police you'll say now! Call them and say what? They make maximum hafta from discos like Magnus. Did I not tell you that one of my best kustomers was an inspector? He was married. He had children. But there he was night after night drinking like a boy from Saudi who had never before seen a girl's face. Best to let it pass. Let it be, I told you, I won't say it again. Why are you staring? Have you never seen a tooth? Are there no teeth in your mouth?!

'Next thing I know you'll run off. And two days after that I'll see you wearing it around your neck on a gold chain! Tsk. I'm only joking baba, I'm joking. Accha, how is Priya? And Chaddi Bhai? He turned out to be an okay fellow. I thought he had got Priya into dhanda, but in the end he took her out of it. The last time we spoke, she was *mast*: eating, drinking, enjoying. She deserves no less. And Apsara? Have you seen my crazy witch of a mother?'

She's fine, I said.

'Of course, she's same-same! The day she changes the sun won't rise!'

Sajida apa walked in, 'Do you girls want to gossip all night, or can we eat dinner as well?'

'Gossip,' Leela mouthed off.

Sajida apa snorted. 'This one is a princess,' she said grimly. 'I tell her to wash the dishes, she says, "But my hands will spoil!" I say, "Cook some food," she says, "But how?" The only thing she knows to do is take a bath. Her bath lasts an hour, and I had to borrow water from the neighbours to cook the meat.'

'Sorry, Sajida apa,' said Leela, looking contrite.

'Sorry doesn't cook meat beti,' Sajida apa pointed out. 'Now come, let's eat. Chit-chat won't fill your stomach.'

5

'Move on. Stay away. Leave me alone'

Leela and Sajida apa could not resolve their differences. Leela was not interested in working in a beauty salon and she wouldn't help around the house. After a few days, a frustrated Sajida apa asked her to leave. Leela returned to Mira Road to the silence of an empty flat. Her bed was perfectly made, her few bits of furniture covered with dust. The unexpected gift of her mother's absence filled her with gratitude. Racing down to Paanwala Shyam's she phoned Priya and asked her to move back in with her immediately.

Priya left Tinkoo. I never saw him again, although on more than one occasion as I drove through Mira Road I thought I saw a boy like him. But in Bombay there were so many boys like him, I could not have been sure.

Leela assumed Apsara had returned to Meerut. But after a few days without news, she decided to ask Paanwala Shyam. He had the ear of Dawood, after all.

'Has she gone home?' Leela asked.

'Arre, what home? She's gone to Malvani,' Paanwala Shyam replied.

Apsara had asked him for advice he said, about starting a bijniss, a bijniss with girls. And he had told her what she needed to know, his fondness for Leela notwithstanding, because he was a bijnissman first. Apsara had paid for the information.

Location was paramount, Paanwala Shyam had informed her, and Malvani was already full of brothels. The police wouldn't care as long as Apsara paid them. 'Hire a room, then hire a dalal,' Paanwala Shyam had said. 'He supplies the first set of girls. Don't get fooled, virgins are half a lakh, you can buy a little girl (not a virgin, mind you) for ten thousand and aunties *toh* are *anda*-bread—cheap and best. If you like foreign what is better than Nepal *ka* maal? The delivery system between the two countries is as smooth as butter.'

'She had an inauspicious start,' Paanwala Shyam confided. 'She paid a dalal twenty-five thousand rupees for three girls. But that night itself, the randis ran off. When she opened their suitcases hoping to recover something she could sell, all she found was kachra.'

Leela wasn't surprised by what her mother had done; she was even a little impressed. 'She's never lived on her own!' she said to me.

She opened a brothel, I reminded her.

Leela shrugged. 'At her age what option does she have?'

She was pleased that Apsara had stolen what she wanted and fled, confirming the worst she had thought of her.

'As long as she stays away,' said Leela. 'I wish her success.'

Still, Apsara was her blood and when she phoned from her new cellphone, inviting me to visit, it was Leela who urged me to go.

∽

Apsara's brothel, a fragile tin-roof construction, squatted above a smoky tea shop that saturated the air with the smell of boiling milk and Glucose biscuits. Up the brief but rickety metal stairs was a short corridor thick with kitchen smoke. A dirty white bra and a blue-and-white mop hung from the same nail.

At the end of this corridor was a small room in which Apsara and two of her girls were seated cross-legged on the floor, watching TV. The girls wore nightdresses and glass bangles; they sat upright and had the appearance of wanting to gobble everything before them.

Apsara was leaning against a bolster and her feet rested

comfortably on the lap of one of the girls, who was massaging them. When she saw me, her face broke into a smile. 'My daughter,' she said, pretending to wipe away tears. 'You came!'

Apsara, I said, sternly.

'You look well, beti,' she said, motioning for me to sit beside her, poking at one of her girls to make space. 'But tell, how do I look?'

Well, I had to admit, settling down.

Apsara had lost weight. Instead of her regulation nightgown, she wore a crisp polyester sari, toe-rings, a Timex. She smelt, refreshingly, of the coconut oil that flattened down her hair and not of stale food or gutka. She looked healthy and not a little smug, her absolute comfort in her surroundings suggesting that she was finally in her natural habitat.

Her new wardrobe matched her new persona. She spoke with an authority I hadn't heard before and it was clear the girls were terrified of her. They called her 'mummy'. She called them 'ai ladki'. As in, 'Ai ladki, if you're not making me money can you at least make me tea?' The one who had been massaging her feet, Monu, scampered off to the kitchen. Setting water to boil, she began to sing Apsara's praises. 'Mummy is like a goddess,' she called out breathlessly. 'She is so pure; she insists we only eat wedge food. Those who want to eat dirty non-wedge must sit outside, she says. And we have to do puja every morning and wash our feet and bottom parts every night. And she lets us take it between our thighs, to save us from children.'

'This one is a tape recorder,' sneered Apsara. 'Anything I say, she repeats.'

Monu blushed.

'She was raped, was she not?' said Apsara. 'So what option but to come into this line? And this one,' she pointed, 'goes by Sonu name. She allowed her boyfriend to give her a baby, did she not? So of course he would not marry her. Marry a slut?'

And now they have you, I said.

'I have taken on the burden,' agreed Apsara.

Sonu stared at the floor. Her feet were bare, her nails long and varnished red.

'Tell what else I said,' Apsara demanded.

Monu peered through the kitchen door, pleased. 'There is only one goddess we should worship,' she said. 'And that is you. And on every festival we should pray to you and give you gifts of money, mithai and saris.'

'Exactly! And if you don't, I'll pluck your eyes out.' Apsara laughed her rasping laugh. 'I'm joking, beti. Tell, tell more.'

'That a woman who sold her daughter to the polis will not hesitate to sell us to ten polis and that a polis only has to see a hole to put it in, and do we know what it's like to be raped non-stop, and if not, would we like to find out, if so we should try running away.'

Apsara gave me a sideways glance. 'Okay okay, enough. Now let mummy talk to her guest.'

Sonu dusted herself off and, jumping up, walked into the kitchen. She leaned over the pot bubbling on the stove. Monu moved over, but kept her eyes trained on Apsara.

I asked Apsara how business was. 'First-class!' she beamed. 'God's grace, after all. Accha, change the channel, *na*. Why we are watching girls dancing nanga-panga? Let's watch a good serial.'

I did as she requested and then sitting back said, Leela is well. She asked about you.

'Volume down,' Apsara called out. Monu scurried over and grabbing the remote control did as asked.

'Beti,' Apsara turned to me, 'can I tell you something?'

I nodded.

'All my life I've lived in someone's shadow, you know that very well. In the shadow of my father. In the shadow of my husband. In the shadows of my sons, my daughter. What does Apsara want to eat? No one asked. What would Apsara like to watch? No one cared. No one cared, because it's not human nature to care for someone dependent on you. But then God, in his mercy, gave me another chance. And look around you, I chose to take it. I have my little bijniss, I make a little money. I'm independent. Well, as independent as an old woman can be! But tell me, how many women my age can say that? Tell me? Most of them die dependant. The clothes they wore, the food they ate, the pillow they slept on, all purchased for them! So do me this favour beti. Tell my daughter everything you saw and all I said. And tell her this: I'm happy. And if she is happy, well then praise God! Finally, we have got what we deserve. Let us forget the past and let each of us, separately, enjoy this present. Tell Leela this for me: Enjoy life, beti. And please, move on. Stay away. Leave me alone.'

I nodded.

She did look happy, I thought. And she deserved to, I supposed. It was not only Leela who had suffered at the hands of Manohar. Leela had suffered terribly, but so had Apsara. And that suffering could only have been compounded by the fact that, unlike Leela, she had never before had the courage to leave.

However Apsara had purchased this new life, at whatever cost, I thought, I hoped she would enjoy it.

Monu brought us tea and as we drank it Apsara touched upon a variety of random subjects: the latest films, the most admirable deity, her favourite chicken recipes. Also, how she was forced to hide her jewellery in a sack of rice to protect it from thieves, and when she said thieves, 'You know who I mean!' she said, swivelling her head to glare at Sonu and Monu.

Later, as I was preparing to leave, she thanked me graciously for visiting her and asked me to visit again.

I knew I wouldn't and I said so.

'In that case,' she replied. 'God bless you, beti. God shower you with blessings.'

Thank you, I said. And good luck to you.

'Don't forget me,' she said.

How could I? I replied, with honesty. You are Leela's mother.
Apsara nodded thoughtfully.
'Yes,' she said. 'I am Leela's mother.'

6

'Once these randis come upstairs, their *chamri* is mine'

O ne weekend Priya spoke of a new boyfriend, an agent who hired bar dancers to perform in clubs in Dubai, and it seemed that it was only the next day when she burst into Leela's flat with the words they had waited so long to hear: 'Contract! Leela, contract!'

Leela was puzzled and, as immediately, she was not. She stared at Priya and as Priya nodded they screamed in unison, 'DUBAI!'

It was a dream come true.

Leela asked if I would accompany her to meet the agent, his name was Sharma. He was older than Priya, he was experienced. He had contacts and, yes, he was vouched for.

By who? I asked.

'Priya of course!' Leela replied.

She anticipated no problems, but wanted me to come along. I agreed and we drove together to a small coffee shop in Borivali West, near the National Park.

Priya was waiting for us and she introduced Sharma with pride. Sharma had a head full of grey hair and a mouth full of gold teeth and he stood over six feet tall.

He was delighted to meet Leela, whom he called 'sister'.

'The sister of my darling!' he said, throwing open his arms.

'The friend of my darling!' he said to me, offering me his hand. He then wiped his hand on his black sherwani and pushed a couple of chairs towards us. 'Sit, please sit,' he said.

Without preamble, he told Leela and Priya that he would

pay them an advance of fifteen thousand rupees and that they would receive Rs. 1.5 lakh for every ninety days of work they did. A single contract generally lasted only ninety days. Once they successfully completed one tour, as he called it, he would set them up on another.

Leela was ecstatic. 'When should I come to the airport?'

Sharma laughed. 'I need to arrange a visit visa for you,' he explained. 'Please grant me a few days, sister.'

She doesn't have a passport, I pointed out.

Sharma smiled benignly. 'No problem. I'll take care of it.'

How?

'Arre! Have I wasted my life working for the bhai *log*? Can I not push through two girls? Don't worry, we have our setting-fitting. We pay the customs people to allow our girls to cross through. Sometimes one of the airports, let us say Bombay, is *garam* because of a terror threat or bhai *log ka* influx-deflux. So we push her through Delhi. She doesn't have to do anything. The customs person has her name, he has been paid. When he registers who she is he simply looks away. She walks on. *Tum bhi* chup, *main bhi* chup. Same thing in abroad.'

'See,' Priya said, pleased. 'Nothing to worry about.'

Leela agreed. 'When can we leave?'

Sharma laughed, 'You girls trust me, but it looks like your friend here does not.'

Priya's mouth hardened.

'No problem, darling,' Sharma patted her. 'We don't have to go. Let me tell you something; I have never before said "yes" to a girl without doing a thorough check-up on her. I met Priya and I said to myself, "Sharma, face it, your darling has a good way of speaking, she has a *mast* figure, why not give her a chance?" Then Priya said, "Not without my sister," and so I agreed to let Leela come along even though we had never before met. I have no regrets, mind you. But usually what happens is this—an agent approaches me, he introduces me to his girl, here, in this same restaurant, in the daytime so I know what I'm buying. I look at

her figure. If she gets a call I listen in. After all, how a girl speaks
to a kustomer, what she says to get him to visit her dance bar
is most important. Sometimes I'm not 100 per cent sure, so I
visit the girl in her dance bar. This was before, mind you. I would
watch how she danced, the quality of kustomer that was drawn
to her, how much money he would throw at her. If I didn't think
she was top-class, foreign-class, I myself would throw five
hundred rupees at her and walk out. Otherwise, I would give
her fifteen thousand, same as I'm going to give you girls, so that
she could pay her expenses and wouldn't come crying to me in
two days' time saying, "I have to pay this bill", "Oh, my mummy
she is so ill." So here I am doing fast-track for you, but if you
are uncomfortable with my generous nature, no problem. Coffee?
Cake-slice? At least have a milkshake, *na*?'

'Amitji has been in bijniss for twenty years,' Priya snapped.

Leela nodded appreciatively, 'And doesn't he look it? He looks
like the big man he is.'

'No problem,' Sharma smiled, petting Priya. 'No problem,
darling. Maybe I was hasty pushy. Just because I'm honest I
assume the best in others. But not everyone is like me. So many
girls I've tried to help have turned out to be fully ganda, total
besharam. They run off with my goodwill advance, even leaving
behind their passports. What do they care? Each of them has
five-six passports. After all, if the bhai *log* can get five-six, why
not the behen *log*?'

'We have full faith in you,' insisted Priya. 'Anyway, we have
no passports, so there's no question of leaving anything behind.'

'And we have no family,' Leela piped in.

'And no friends,' she added for good measure. 'Even if we
wanted to, where would we go, you tell?'

Sharma's eyes gleamed. 'I'm sure you have family. You must
have friends.'

'No,' Leela said firmly. 'Only the people at this table.'

'We would never run away,' Priya said. 'We are orphans, in
God's hands. And in your hands too.'

Sharma smiled. 'Order something *na*? My treat I told, order anything you want. Sharma is best host is what you should be thinking at all times.'

He turned to me, suddenly genial. What did I matter? I was the ugly sister to his Cinderellas.

'Too bad we had to meet in daytime, because of bijniss,' he said, all friendly. 'Nighttime is when we bhai *log* have our fun. Just this week we had dinner inside the National Park. You know the National Park? You know how they say, "No make fire!" "No shoot animals!" But do we care? We have our setting! We made a fire, we roasted a whole goat, a few big-big multi-colourful birds. We got full drunk! A daru maker had passed by with his drum, you see. What did we do? Same as always! We pulled him to the fire. Poor fellow passed *peshab*, so hard he was begging for his life. We threw him to a side. "We don't want your peshab," I said. "But your daru? That we'll gladly drink!"'

Priya preened, 'I *told* you he's a big man!'

Sharma pretended to demur, 'No, no, darling, I am only a small fellow. The great one is God. No one is greater than God, remember that.'

'God is great,' agreed Leela.

'Amitji, you are too modest,' Priya said. 'Tell them everything. They are my sisters.'

Leela nodded persuasively, 'It's not often we get to meet men like you, Amitji. Usually, it's tapori *log*. There are only small people in our little world.'

Sharma grinned. 'Well . . .'

'Please tell no.'

Sharma turned to me. 'You know me.'

Definitely not, I said.

'What if I said the name Abu Salem?'

Abu Salem was the notorious gangster whose girlfriend Priya's customer had insisted I looked like. He had started in Bombay in the 1980s as a taxi driver, but was soon gun-running for

Dawood. At the time of his arrest later that year, he was impli-
cated in over sixty cases of murder, as well as in dozens of cases
of extortion and kidnapping.

Please don't say you're siblings, I thought.

'What if I said I'm *that* Amit Sharma? The Amit Sharma who
was, you know,' Sharma wiggled his right hand, 'Salem's right-
hand man?'

Leela bounced. 'I know you, I know you! You're that Amit
Sharma?'

Sharma nodded, pleased. 'The same.'

I hadn't heard of him and was quite sure Leela hadn't either.
But I stayed quiet. Priya's boyfriend was a gangster! Gangsters
carried guns!

∽

'Ah, now you've made me nostalgic,' said Sharma. 'Those were
the days I tell you, our days in Dubai. Salem loved women.
Organizers would visit his mansion with a photo album of bar
dancers they were planning to bring over. Salem would carefully
go through each and every album. How the organizers would
rattle in their shoes! "Bhai, they're beautiful right? Bhai, worth
it no?" Salem would almost always nod and the organizers would
exhale with relief. If he liked a girl, he would want to make sure
she made it to Dubai. So he would ask, "Theek *hai*? *Ya ek do*
peti *doon*?" Are you okay for money, or should I give you a
couple of lakhs? The day before the troupe began work, Salem
would drop by for a preview. The bar was locked behind him.
He got the best seat, of course. The girls would take to the floor,
their eyes trained on him. For effect, I would sometimes hand
him a cell and urge him to take the call. With a motion of his
hand he would make the music stop and bark loudly into the
phone: "Pump his body with bullets! I want him to die like a
dog on the road. Then call for an ambulance. And run it over
his body!" How impressed those girls would get! How big their
eyes would become! If Salem wanted one of them, I would phone

the bar the next day and order the manager to release her. I would pick her up before the evening's show and drop her off at Sharjah, the guest house Salem rented for meetings. A few hours later, after the girl had given him whatever made him happy, he would call me over and say to me, "Amit, take her to Ashok Jeweller's and buy her whatever she wants." When the girl's attention was diverted, he would motion with his fingers— one for one *tola*, two for two tolas of gold—the value of the gift he wished to give.'

'What a generous man!' exclaimed Leela.

'If he liked you,' Sharma conceded. 'If you upset him, mind it, there was no saying what he would do. I remember clearly how one organizer upset him terribly. He refused to let Salem have one of his girls, the fool! The organizer placed the blame on someone else: "Gurubhai," he lied, "I *want* to send her to you, but her agent threatened to ruin me if I did." A few days later, that agent, Tipu was his name, I still remember, he was walking towards his home in Kandivali when someone came up behind him and slit his throat with a razor blade. Blood every-where, I heard, flowing like the Ganga! What an impact it had! For a month organizers were terrified to enter Dubai. How bijniss suffered! Come to think of it, these things were fairly common then.'

Murder? I said.

'Arre! But why say no to begin with? Didn't Salem pay for what he took? Did anyone ever leave his bed without a gift? Always a gold ornament, a handycam, a watch. He was so generous! Of course, he didn't like the talkers. Or the thieves. If a girl kept on about her mummy who was sick or her brother pestering her to buy him jeans-pant from Dubai, he would get fed up. Or if he noticed that a girl had stolen one of the perfumes from his bathroom cabinet, he would say to me, "Arre Amit, make sure I don't see her face again."'

'So the less we speak the better?' Leela said, as though taking notes.

'I'll give you a tip,' Sharma replied. 'And I won't charge for it. You're going to Dubai to earn money, are you not?'

The girls nodded.

'So why talk? Hahn, talk on the phone in such a way that a man goes mad in his desire to see you, even if it is only to watch you dance from a distance of twenty feet. But once you have him in your control, for God's sake, keep quiet!'

'I don't mind,' said Leela. 'No problem.'

'Trust me,' said Sharma. 'I know what I'm talking. Do you know how I got into this bijniss? Let me tell you. I spent my childhood running in and out of jail. I was such a harami, I had no choice but to approach a Company man. "Bhai, find some use for me," I pleaded. And he did. First I was a doorman at a dance bar and then one night I was made the lookout during a robbery. After that, I became Dawood's muscle man. I swallowed my pride even though I came from a good family, even though I had some school learning. Whatever the job, however much the maar-peet, I said, all the bhais started this way. Haji Mastan was a coolie. Abu Salem a driver. Once I had proved myself, Salem chose me as his top man. And I remained his top man, even after he left Dawood. That's when we went upstairs to Dubai, to start afresh. I remember those days like it was yesterday. How did we eat? Salem would put in twenty dirhams, his wife Sameera would put in ten and the rest of us would pitch in a few dirhams each, whatever we could. What days those were, what adventures we had! My ears were so close to the ground I could hear the sewer gushing!'

So why are you out here while Salem is on the run? I said.

'Because he's a brave man,' Priya snapped.

Sharma shrugged, 'I'm a *khabru*.' A snitch.

'So what! You're a brave khabru. If it wasn't for you how your poor wife would suffer! And your daughter? The little angel would cry herself to sleep every single night!'

'True, I did it for them,' Sharma said soberly. 'For their honour, I admit. I couldn't ask my wife to spend the next ten years of her life bringing me dal-chawal in jail, could I? And what option did I have? The police caught me at Delhi airport as I was leaving for Dubai and they said to me either I go with them or I go to jail. Which would I prefer? "Fine," I said. So here I am, waiting to speak out against my boss. In the murder of Pradeep Jain, the builder who was killed in 1995, in the murder of Ajit Dewan. He was the secretary of that actress, Manisha Koirala—know her? What have I got to lose when Salem finds out? Only my life.'

'Don't lose your life,' Leela giggled nervously.

'Not before you send us to Dubai,' said Priya with a coy smile.

'No one can kill me,' Sharma boasted. 'See this.' Rolling up his sleeve, he pointed to a deep scar on his right arm. It was perhaps eight or nine inches long and ran from his elbow to his wrist. 'They came to my house to murder me. To my house! No respect! Guess my response? Of course, I stabbed all three of them, and whose fault was it that one died?'

'Amitji went to jail,' Priya said with awe.

'Priya understands me,' Sharma acknowledged, with another tap on her shoulder. 'Why just her? There's a natural bond between bar dancers and bhai *log*. Who else will help them?'

'They are the best!' Priya agreed.

'Kasam *se*!' Leela nodded, happily.

'Soniaji,' Sharma leaned in. 'I know you're worried. I can see it in your face. So let me tell you how we work. Then you decide for yourself, okay?'

'But there's nothing left to decide,' Priya cried.

Sharma hushed her. 'Let me talk. And let me be honest . . . Now let's say there's a bar girl. Let's call her Sonia. Sonia has a devoted kustomer. He comes to the bar every night. He takes her phone number. He likes her, she pretends to like him. Soon she knows everything about him. *Do* numberwala, paisawala, smuggler. One day she takes him into her confidence and says, "Look, the money you throw on me only goes to the boss. If you really love me send this money to my parents instead." So the kustomer does just that. Through hawala.'

Hawala was an illegal, informal system of laundering money into foreign currencies.

'Now instead of coming to the bar he talks to Sonia on her cell. One day passes, two days pass, where's Sonia's kustomer? Why isn't she making money for me? So I get her roommate to listen in on her conversations. Remember this: the organizer is boss. Girls are on their toes at the chance to get close to him. So the girl gladly listens in. Soon she comes to me and whispers, "Sonia still talks to that fellow." I call my bhai *log*. I find out that several hawalas were sent to Bombay in Sonia's name. That's it, game over. I take her phone card. Her kustomer goes crazy trying to talk to her. Finally, he comes to the bar. Sonia tells him what happened. He crawls over to me. "Bhai, give her phone card back," he begs. "Let her talk to me bhai, and I'll keep coming to the bar, God swear." I ignore him. He comes back the next evening and spends money. The evening after that, he spends more money. A few more evenings pass, Sonia's friend keeps sinking money into the bar. At that point, I let Sonia have her phone card back. She has learnt her lesson. From now on, she will cut that man's throat from one corner to the next until he has bled all his money into the bar. If after this Sonia is a good girl, if she makes me at least five lakh rupees, then when she has ten days left before she has to go back to Bombay, I make her free. You want to go to kustomer's flat? Go. You want me to send a guard with you? Done. Kustomer gave you a gold chain and earrings and you say, "Bhai, please let me keep this, please, please don't take it away from me," no problem. You made me money, now I will let you make money. Otherwise, stay locked up for those ten days and learn your lesson.'

'So in those ten days we can do anything we like?' Leela asked.

'Anything,' Sharma replied, magnanimously. 'Your body is your own after all. Go meet your kustomers, get them to bathe you in dirhams, to buy presents for you, your mummy and your friends, as you wish.'

Priya was pleased. 'Like before.'

She reached out for Leela's hand. Leela flashed her a smile. I hadn't see her so happy in a long time.

'Touch up?' she said.

∽

The girls reached for their handbags and walked away clasping each other tightly around the waist.

Sharma watched them with open interest. He turned his face towards mine. I thought he was going to ask if I wanted a cup of coffee.

'One thing,' he said. 'One thing I didn't mention.'

What's that? I asked.

'Just this. *Ki* once these randis come upstairs, their *chamri* belongs to me.'

I stared. You will own them? Is that what you're saying?

'Own?' said Sharma sitting up. 'Is that what you call bijniss? Arre madam, ghoda *ghas se dosti karega to khayega kya*? If a horse befriends the grass what will he eat? This is not owner-ship, Soniaji; this is life.'

Sharma sighed. 'These Dubai trips, they last two years, max three. The first time your Leela sleeps with her kustomer he will give her a bracelet. After that she will get a chain. After that, cash. But after that all she will get is talk. Because once your Leela becomes familiar, as familiar as a wife, a girlfriend, she will get nothing, exact as a wife or girlfriend. And once her kustomer loses interest, naturals, so will I. That is naturals. Then no more Dubai for your Leela. So what will your Leela do? No, no, let me tell you. Let me tell you because I have seen this for fifteen years. Fifteen years, with my own eyes! Maybe she's told you she wants to open a booty parlour, do fashion? Am I right? Or did she say, "I'll try my luck in films"? Or wait, did she say, "I want to find a good man"? Right? But let me tell you what will really happen. Once your Leela is no longer welcome in Dubai, she will be at a loss. How to earn? How to eat? She is old now, after all. So this is what she will do: she will invest whatever money her mother hasn't stolen from her into a flat. She will spend two, maybe three, lakhs, buy a place in Mira Road, Bhayander, Thane, someplace like that. And with that flat, she will get girls into this line. Unless she has a daughter. If a kustomer gives her a daughter she is set. She will sell her daughter, even if she is her only child, her only family, because her mother sold her and who is her daughter to deserve better?'

Just because it's true for many bar dancers doesn't mean it will be true for Leela, I said. Leela may want something else.

Sharma smiled.

The girls were walking back. Priya was on her cellphone, Leela looked ahead. She raised her right hand and, winking, fluttered it at me.

Hello?

Bye bye?

'True fact,' Sharma was saying. 'Leela may want something else.'

He leaned back and, yawning, stretched his hands above his head. 'Leela may want something else. But who will permit Leela what she wants?'

7

'Tell me, do you see it?'

Leela reminded me she was going abroad and asked if I would drive her to the airport. She was flying with Priya to Delhi and they would make their onward journey with a friend of Sharma's, 'to be safe'. She had no second thoughts, she said. Sharma had been trying to impress me into believing he was a big don. He was no Bada Don. He was a khabru, a cunt, a failed crossing away from being a chamar chor. Leela and Priya had saved his career! She knew the Sharmas of the world. They talked fast and loose. As though anyone could own her—her! Remember, she said gently, a bar dancer's game is *lootna*, kustomer *ko* bewakuf *banana*. And a kustomer was any man she would meet, don't take tension.

You're not going to Night Lovers, I said. In Dubai they may do things differently.

'Don't worry,' she insisted. 'I'll be in touch, God promise. Accha, I'll send you a postcard. I'll go to Wild Wadi and be *mast* enough for us both. I'll go to Jumeirah Beach! I'll do shopping, so much shopping I'll do! I'll eat gold!'

Okay, I said.

Leela shook her head as though to say, 'Will you never learn?'

She held out her hand. 'Come here. Look at me.'

I obliged.

Leela had lost weight, she was thinner than when we had first met. But she appeared small too, diminished.

'Look properly,' she insisted, standing still.

Leela patted her hair away from her face and flashed me a smile.

What am I looking for? I asked.

'Fear,' she said.

'Tell me, do you see it?'

I didn't have to think twice.

No, I said. I don't think I ever have.

Acknowledgements

This is a work of non-fiction, researched and written over a period of five years. To understand the world of the bar dancers I conducted hundreds of interviews across Bombay. Among the people I met with were bar dancers, bar owners, customers, stewards, waiters, sex workers, hijras, brothel madams, gangsters, policemen of all ranks from the then commissioner of police to constables on the street, politicians, lawyers representing both the bar dancers and the bar owners in their lawsuit against the State of Maharashtra, NGO workers, media persons and the families of women working in the bar line. To protect the identity of the people involved, I have, with the exception of public figures, changed all names and identifying characteristics of people and places. While I was present for most of the events described in this book, some dialogue and characters were reconstructed.

I would like to dedicate this book to the people who gave me their time and shared with me their stories. This is for you. Thank you.

I consulted with numerous people during the writing of this book, and in particular I'd like to thank Kamlesh Singh, Deepak Rao, Deepti Priya Mehrotra, Manjit Singh Sethi, Laxminarayan Tripathi, Penny Richards, Ashish Khetan, Sandeep Pendse, Alok Gupta, Vikram Doctor and Veena Gowda. To Ravi Singh and Meru Gokhale—I couldn't have asked for more involved and painstaking editors; thank you so much. To my early readers Ulrik McKnight, Chiki Sarkar and Amit Varma; to Prabha Desai and her indefatigable staff at the Sanmitra Trust (Goregaon and Malvani), to Nikita Lalwani, Ulla McKnight, Sanjiv Valsan and Negar Akhavi, my deepest thanks. To Shobhaa Dé, this was your idea: Thank you. Gregory David Roberts, thank you for your encouragement and support; it means so much. And to my agent Tracy Bohan at the Wylie Agency, for her enthusiasm and support, all my thanks.